THE DIGNITY OF MAN

An Islamic Perspective

Mohammad Hashim Kamali

THE DIGNITY OF MAN

An Islamic Perspective

ISLAMIC TEXTS SOCIETY

This edition published 2002 by The Islamic Texts Society
22a Brooklands Avenue, Cambridge CB2 2DQ, U.K.

ISBN 1 903682 00 2 paper
ISBN 1 903682 03 7 cloth

First published 1999 by Ilmiah Publishers, Kuala Lumpur, Malaysia

British Library Cataloguing in Publication Data
A catalogue record for this book is available from the British Library

ABOUT THE AUTHOR

Dr. Mohammad Hashim Kamali is Professor of Law at the International Islamic University of Malaysia, where he has been teaching Islamic law and jurisprudence since 1985. Born in Afghanistan in 1944, he studied law at Kabul University, where he was later appointed Assistant Professor. Following this he worked as Public Attorney with the Ministry of Justice in Afghanistan. He completed his LL.M. and his doctoral studies at London University, where he specialised in Islamic law and Middle Eastern Studies. Dr. Kamali then held the post of Assistant Professor at the Institute of Islamic Studies at McGill University in Montreal, and later worked as a Research Associate with the Social Science and Humanities Research Council of Canada. He is the author of *Law in Afghanistan. A Study of the Constitutions, Matrimonial Law and the Judiciary* (Leiden: E.J. Brill, 1985); *Principles of Islamic Jurisprudence* (second edition, Cambridge: The Islamic Texts Society, 1991); *Freedom of Expression in Islam* (Kuala Lumpur: Berita, 1994; new edition, Cambridge: The Islamic Texts Society, 1997); *Punishment in Islamic Law: an Enquiry into the Ḥudūd Bill of Kelantan* (Kuala Lumpur: Institute for Policy Research, 1995); *Istiḥsān (Juristic Preference) and its Application to Contemporary Issues* (Jeddah: Islamic Research and Training Institute, Eminent Scholars Lecture Series No. 20, 1997) and numerous articles in reputable international journals. He is twice recipient of the Ismāʿīl al-Fārūqī Award for Academic Excellence in 1995 and 1997. Dr. Kamali whishes to acknowledge that he prepared the present edition of this book during his stay at the Institute for Advanced Study, Berlin, where he was a fellow for the academic year 2000-2001.

بسم الله الرحمن الرحيم

Contents

Introduction

Human rights are a manifestation of human dignity. Constitutional proclamations on the rights of the citizen are a way of upholding the dignity and worth of the human person. Rights and liberties that are inherent in humanity, such as freedom, equality, and the right to personal safety, as well as those that are acquired as a result of human effort, such as ownership, are all rooted in human dignity. 'Human rights', as the UN Secretary General Kofi Annan pointed out, 'assert the dignity of each and every individual human being, and the inviolability of the individual's rights. They belong inherently to each person, each individual, and are not conferred by or subject to any governmental authority.'[1] From the Islamic perspective, dignity is a manifestation of God's favour on mankind. Yet the concepts of right, human rights, and of human dignity are not entirely objective and value-free as they are often read in the context of tradition, public opinion, and culture. A Confucian might see right and order as a question of 'good manners, propriety and consideration for others'; a Hindu might see them another way; and the Western perception of human rights is predominantly individualist as it is focused on individual claims and privileges to the neglect, sometimes, of individual responsibilities and obligations. The Universal Declaration of Human Rights (UDHR) has often been criticised for its neglect of community rights, and also for being seen as less than universal in that it is rooted mainly in Western values and culture. Formulated in the wake of World War II by the dominant military powers who colonised most of the remaining parts of the earth, the Declaration was drafted in a language and style that did not fully reflect the concerns of non-Western peoples.

The bewildering devastation of World War II had prompted concern that such atrocities should never happen again, and hence the emergence of the ideology of human rights, which became, for the first time, an engaging theme of international concern. Unlike 'civil rights' or 'minority rights', the idea of human rights implied universality, ascribing to all individuais certain inalienable rights by virtue of their humanity. Following World War II, individuals and civic organisations campaigned to establish an international bill of rights, and the Universal Declaration of Human Rights was adopted by the United Nations General Assembly on 10 December 1948.

The divisive policies of Nazi Germany and Imperial Japan were discredited in the post-World War II period and belief in the emergence of a global community with common allegiance to human rights was gaining ground. In the United States, an unprecedented movement for 'one world' and a spirit of unity that blended the philosophies and cultures of East and West had emerged. Global unity was seen as an even more urgent necessity, because of the threat of atomic war, and many believed that humanity faced the choice of 'one world or none'.

There was at the time much debate on the philosophical tendencies and cultural influences that were reflected in the Declaration. Human rights activists sought to demonstrate a cross-cultural basis for the underlying values of the Declaration. The UN Educational, Scientific and Cultural Organisation (UNESCO) had in 1948 disseminated a volume of essays on human rights perspectives in Islam, Hinduism, Marxism and Confucianism. The UN General Assembly deliberations on the Declaration had also seen attempts by participating countries to remove the imprint of the natural law theory on the Document. The initial draft of the Declaration's first article, which stated that human beings were endowed with rights 'by nature', was removed to avoid philosophical disagreement on the origin of rights. Article (1) was then amended to read that, 'All human beings were born free and equal in dignity and rights. They are endowed with reason and conscience and should act towards one another in a spirit of brotherhood.' The consensus, after much debate, was that philosophical agreement could not be reached but that member countries should arrive at a practical agreement on a bill of rights that would help individuals and peoples fight oppression. In the final vote on the Declaration, no country voted against it, except the Soviet Union and several Communist states, and Saudi Arabia abstained. Saudi Arabia, Pakistan, Egypt and several other Muslim countries objected to Article (18) of the Declaration which guaranteed freedom to change one's religion. But this argument was challenged not by Western diplomats, but by a divergent voice from within the Muslim World. Zafrullah Khan, the then Foreign Minister of Pakistan, advocated the view, quoting the Qur'ān, that Islam recognised the right to conversion, and ultimately persuaded every Muslim country, except Saudi Arabia, to vote in favour of the Declaration. Even Saudi Arabia, despite its abstention in the final vote, had not objected to the principle of human rights as a whole. It had, in fact, contributed to the discussions in the General Assembly at one point where the Declaration's reference to everyone's entitlement to 'social security' in Article (22) was to be replaced by 'social justice' because of the clear correspondence of the latter phrase with Islamic principles.

More recently the view has been expressed by a number of Asian governments in various international events that some human rights are undoubtedly universal, but there are other human rights that are founded on the Western ideal of individual autonomy and do not accord with 'Asian values'. It was also said that the UDHR had been drawn up without their participation and so it was not truly universal. It was further stated that in the absence of economic development and social stability, emphasis on civil and political rights in the developed countries would be inappropriate.

These views were reflected in the Bangkok Declaration, which was adopted in March 1993 by the Asian States, prior to the Vienna World Conference on Human Rights held later in the same year. The Bangkok Declaration provided in Article(8) that 'while human rights are universal in nature, they must be considered in the context of [...] national and regional particularities and various historical, cultural and religious backgrounds'.

Human rights in the West are seen primarily in the context of the relationship of citizen and state, a relic of their historical origin as claims articulated by the bourgeoisie in the modern West against absolutist states. Although the concept of human rights has in the twentieth century expanded to include collective rights as well as social and economic rights, these additions have not changed the view of human rights as claims that citizens make upon their states. This premise seems to be somewhat oblivious of the growing recognition that non-state parties such as warlords, tribal and guerrilla groups can also violate human rights. Moreover, there is yet insufficient recognition, let alone consensus, on the degree to which more powerful agents of international systems, whether dominant governments, multinational corporations, fund managers and currency speculators, also can and do violate human rights. The question may also be asked as to how the Declaration attends to the emerging global system, and the increasing menace of globalisation to individuals, less powerful communities and states? Can the language of the Declaration be applied to the relationship between individuals and global political and financial systems? Do issues of global concern, such as economic imbalance and a fair distribution of resources fall within the scope of the Declaration? As one observer commented on the fiftieth anniversary of the UDHR, 'the international order remains a much unbalanced one, dominated by Western industrialised powers. This is true of the UN itself as well as of multilateral organisations like the International Monetary Fund, World Health Organisation, etc.'[2] Another commentator posed the following questions: 'Do individuals in Asia and Africa have the right to protest the blatantly undemocratic representation of the UN Security Council? Can citizens of the international community argue that nuclear weapons—not just in India, Pakistan or North Korea, but also in the United States, home to half the World's arsenal—threaten their rights to life and security?'[3] It seems that the theory of human rights has not evolved to keep pace with the course of changes since its inception. Daim Zainuddin has observed that the fundamentals that influenced the Declaration should be reviewed. When the Declaration was proclaimed in 1948, there were only about forty members in the United Nations. Today, there are more than 180 members. He added, however, that the present Declaration is not fundamentally flawed, only that 'the passage of time and the emergence of new situations and issues necessitate the formulation of a new declaration or a major overhaul of the present declaration'.[4]

Cumaraswamy has expounded the opposite view to the effect that the relativist position that questions the universality of the UDHR is inconsistent in the sense that most of the member states have subsequently accepted and ratified the Declaration. Quoted in support of this view is the resolutions of the June 1993 World Conference on Human Rights in Vienna where some 171 Member States of the UN participated and clearly upheld 'the universality of human rights and argued that cultural and religious traditions did not constitute an obstacle to the realisation of international human rights norms'.[5]

When states accept human rights as expounded in the UDHR and other supportive documents, they still need to deal with the delicate task of interpreting and applying these rights in local contexts. The implementation of international human rights norms are thus inevitably conditioned by the historical, cultural and social particularities of the countries concerned. This, however, 'does not deny or diminish the importance of the principle of universality of human rights as enshrined in the 1948 Declaration'.[6] It thus appears that the two views are not necessarily in conflict. The advocates of the relativist view seem to be mainly concerned with the implementation of the UDHR and a certain recognition of the local context for enforcement, while accepting in principle the universalist calibre of human rights. The relativist view does not therefore necessarily deny the universalist approach. Musa Hitam, the leader of the Malaysian delegation to the UN Commission on Human Rights, has noted that it was admittedly the victors of the war who dominated the framing of the Declaration, and that the 'world' as it was then is not the world as it is now. He adds that 'it would be wrong, however, to say that for this reason alone the Declaration could not be acceptable or be relevant'.[7]

Islam's perception of human rights is not premised on the individual versus nation-state framework. The nation-state itself represents a superimposition which has little claim to authenticity in the authoritative sources of Islam, namely the Qur'ān and *Sunnah*. The Qur'ān and *Sunnah* lend support to the creation of a political order and leadership that takes charge of community affairs and administers justice. But the main actor and audience in all this is the individual, not the state. The Qur'ān also addresses the individual and the community of believers when it speaks of the duty of *ḥisbah*, that is, the 'promotion of good and prevention of evil' (*amr bi'l-maʿrūf wa nahy ʿan al-munkar*). The community of believers, the *ummah*, is consistently addressed in the Qur'ān as 'O you who believe', that is, the plurality of individual believers, not a separate or corporate body of its own. The individual is required to obey the *ulū al-amr*, that is, persons who are entrusted with leadership but who are accountable to the community. The whole conception of Islamic political organisation and the state is service-oriented and humanitarian in the sense that the individual remains the principal actor in all its parts. The state as a corporate entity is not the primary actor, nor is it the repository of supreme political authority. The *ummah* or the community of believers, is the *locus* of political authority, which is often described as a form of executive sovereignty. This is a delegated sovereignty that is founded in the Qur'ānic doctrine of the vicegerency of man on earth, that is, the *khilāfah*. It is by virtue of this derived, or delegated, sovereignty that the community is seen as the repository of political power.

Islam has devised a unitary system of law and government in which ultimate sovereignty belongs only to God. Both the individual and the state are subject to the same law and their basic rights and duties are predetermined by the *Sharīʿah*. The objectives of justice, promotion of benefit (*maṣlaḥah*) and prevention of corruption and harm (*mafsadah*), are to be pursued by both, and the state has no authority to overrule or replace the *Sharīʿah*, or to violate any of its principles. Thus the duality of interests between the individual and state envisaged in the modern theory of human rights does not present a dominant source of concern for the Muslim jurists. The jurists and *ʿulamā'* did not proceed on the assumption that the interests of the individual and state were potentially in conflict. The view has prevailed instead that Islam assumes a basic harmony between the individual and state, which is to be realised through the implementation of the *Sharīʿah*. This is a consequence partly of the Qur'ānic doctrine of unicity (*tawḥīd*), which has profoundly influenced Islamic thought and institutions. When the state succeeds in enforcing the *Sharīʿah*, it satisfies the basic purpose of its existence. Since individual and state are expected to subscribe to the same set of values, and the state exists in order to administer justice, no necessary conflict is assumed to exist between the rights of the individual and the state power.

A similar scenario can be visualised with regard to modern constitutional law, which resembles the theory of human rights in that both are predicated on the duality of interests between the individual and state. Constitutionalism as a phenomenon emerged and developed on the assumption that the nation-state presented a menace to the rights and liberties of the citizen. These rights were potentially in conflict with state power and its relentless drive to control the lives and activities of its citizens. Constitutional law was then developed in the West as an instrument for regulating this conflict. More recently, however, this perception of duality in the fabric of constitutional law has also been questioned and there has been growing recognition of the view that the state is a potential ally and protector of civil rights and liberties. This shift in the underlying perception of constitutional law would, in turn, seem to require parallel changes in the theory and practice of constitution in the nation-states as they stand, something which has evidently not yet materialised and which present a fresh challenge for future reform of constitutional law.

Islam's perception of leadership and political power that administers the affairs of the community is inherently individualist in the sense that leaders are committed to serve the best interests of the individual. The state is under duty to protect the five essential interests (i.e. *al-ḍarūriyāt al-khamsah*), namely, faith, life, property, intellect and lineage, through the establishment of a just political order and government. The Qur'ān has proclaimed human dignity an inherent right of the individual in an absolute and unqualified sense, as discussed below, and this then provides a matrix for the rest of his basic rights.

When human rights are seen as a manifestation of respect for human dignity, human rights are likely to have a more authentic basis across cultural traditions. As one commentator noted, 'nothing could be more important than to underscore and defend the dignity of the human person'.[8] To take dignity as the goal and purpose of human rights would be to enrich the calibre and substance of these rights.

Islam's perception of human rights is rooted in human dignity and it is, at the same time, intertwined with human obligation. Obligation is a primary concept, indeed the main focus, of the *Sharīʿah*, and it often takes priority over right. Indeed, it is through the acceptance and fulfilment of obligations that individuals acquire certain rights. Dignity thus becomes a reality when there is a balanced emphasis on rights and obligations.

World cultures and traditions tend to differ not only in the value-content of human rights but in regard to many other variables that influence the place and priority that is given to those rights. The Western tradition posits freedom in order mainly to avoid the outcome of a despotic system of government, while Islam emphasises virtue as a goal for both the individual and society. The West emphasises individual rights and interests, while Islam gives priority to collective good in the event where the latter conflicts with the interest of the individual. Having said this, the individual still remains the primary agent and focus of attention in Islamic law.

The Qur'ān is expressive of the dignity of man in numerous places and a variety of contexts, including the image that it conveys of the physical aspects of man's creation, his spiritual ranking, and the affirmation of God's love for mankind. The Qur'ān is also expressive of the dignity of man in its proclamations on man's appointment as God's vicegerent on earth, the subjugation of the created universe and its resources to man's benefit and service, and the protective and punitive measures that are designed to safeguard human dignity. Social decorum and dignified encounter, just and upright character, safeguards against physical abuse, and protection against poverty and degradation are some of the other areas where Islam provides substance to its perception of human dignity. The *Sunnah* of the Prophet also provides the authority for protecting the dignity of the dead in almost the same manner as that of the living. These are some of the themes that are elaborated in the following pages. But one of the basic postulates that this work develops in some detail is that of God's love as the cause of the creation of man and of the conferment of dignity on him. Man's dignity is, in other words, an affirmation of God's love for human beings. Any discussion on human dignity in Islam needs, therefore, to begin with a survey of Qur'ānic declarations on the subject.

NOTES

1. Quoted in a feature article in *The Star*, 'Weighing Our Rights and Freedoms', 10 December 1998, Section 2, p. 3.
2. Francis Loh, 'Striving to Reach Ideals', *The Star*, 10 December 1998, Section 2, p. 5.
3. Shirin Sinnar, 'Reflection on the 50th Anniversary of the Universal Declaration of Human Rights', *Commentary: International Movement for a Just World* (Kuala Lumpur), new series, no. 19 (December 1998), p. 4.
4. Quoted in Param Cumaraswamy, 'The Universal Declaration of Human Rights—Is it Universal?', *Insaf: The Journal of the Malaysia Bar*, XXVI, no. 4 (December 1997), p. 39.
5. Ibid., p. 42.
6. Ibid., p. 43.
7. Interview with Musa Hitam, *The Star*, 10 December 1998, Section 2, p. 3.
8. Raimondo Pannikar, 'Is the Notion of Human Rights a Western Concept?', *Interculture* (Montreal), vol. 17, no. 1 (March 1982), p. 28.

CHAPTER ONE

The Qur'ānic View of Human Dignity

The Qur'ānic vision of human dignity is manifested in various ways and in different contexts. To begin with, we read the direct and unqualified affirmation of the dignity of man in the following Qur'ānic text, where God Most High declares:

> We have bestowed dignity on the progeny of Adam [...] and conferred on them special favours, above a great part of Our creation. (al-Isrā', 17:70)
>
> ولقد كرمنا بنى آدم [...] وفضلناهم على كثير ممّن خلقنا تفضيلاً.

The text here is self-evident and comprehensive in its recognition of dignity for all human beings without limitations or qualifications of any kind. Thus according to al-Alusī (d. 1270/1854), 'everyone and all members of the human race, including the pious and the sinner, are endowed with dignity, nobility and honour, which cannot be exclusively expounded and identified. Ibn ᶜAbbās, the Companion of the Prophet Muḥammad ﷺ famed for his Qur'ānic exegesis, has commented, however, that God Most High has honoured mankind by endowing him with the faculty of reason.'[1]

Dignity in other words is not earned by meritorious conduct; it is an expression of God's favour and grace. Muṣṭafā al-Sibāᶜī and Ḥasan al-ᶜĪlī have similarly remarked that dignity is a proven right of every human being regardless of colour, race or religion.[2] Aḥmad Yusrī has drawn the conclusion that 'dignity is established for every human being as of the moment of birth'.[3] Sayyid Quṭb has similarly stated that dignity is the natural right of every individual. The children of Adam have been honoured not for their personal attributes or status in society, but for the fact that they are human beings. 'Dignity is therefore the absolute right of everyone.'[4] Al-Zuḥaylī has similarly noted that 'dignity is the natural right (*ḥaqq ṭabīʿī*) of every human being. Islam has upheld it as such and made it a principle of government and a criterion of interaction (*al-muʿāmalah*) among people.' It is not permissible to violate the personal dignity of anyone, regardless of whether the person is pious or of ill-repute, Muslim or non-Muslim. Even a criminal is entitled to dignified treatment. For punishment is meant to be for retribution and reform, not indignity and humiliation.[5] Most of these commentators have made reference, in addition to the clear text of the Qur'ān, to the *ḥadīth* that records the incident where the Prophet ﷺ saw a funeral procession passing by; upon seeing it, he rose in respect and remained standing until one of his Companions informed him that the deceased person was a Jew. This intervention provoked the Prophet's disapproval as he posed the question, 'Was he not a human being?'[6] The Prophet ﷺ, in other words, did not consider the religious following of the deceased person to have any bearing on his inherent dignity, which called for unqualified respect. Muḥammad al-Ghazālī has quoted Ibn Ḥazm to the effect that a Christian woman, Umm al-Ḥārith bint Abī Rabīʿah, died and the Prophet's Companions took part in her funeral procession.[7] Al-Ghazālī then concluded that 'we would like to see that our relations with other communities are founded on this kind of latitude (*al-samāḥah*). This is because we believe that Islam commands us to have good and peaceful relations with those who are not aggressive toward us'.[8] The Qur'ānic declaration under review has also prompted Weeramantry to observe that the Qur'ān makes dignity intrinsic to the personality of every individual so that 'no regime, however powerful, could take it away from him'. This inherent human dignity also 'provides the basis of modern doctrines of human rights'.[9]

The Qur'ānic declaration of dignity for the whole of the human race in the foregoing *āyah* has, in another place, been more specifically endorsed with reference to the Muslims. The dignified status (*al-ʿizzah*) of the believers is thus expounded alongside that of God Most High and His Messenger, Muḥammad ﷺ:

> And honour belongs to God, to His Messenger and the believers. (al-Munāfiqūn, 63:8)

وللّه العزة ولرسوله وللمؤمنين.

On a more general note, the Prophet ﷺ declared in a *ḥadīth* that 'people are God's children and those dearest to God are the ones who treat His children kindly'.[10]

الناس عيال اللّه، أحبهم الى اللّه أرحمهم لعياله.

The Qur'ān and *Sunnah* normally refer to people as God's servants (*ʿibād Allāh*), but here they are elevated to the status of God's beloved children, which naturally conveys a more dignified status.

In the physical world according to the worldview of Islam, there is no place on earth holier than the House of God, the Kaʿba. Yet the Prophet ﷺ drew the following parallel to express the extent of the dignity of the believers. The Prophet ﷺ, while facing the Kaʿba, said:

> You are most pure and most dignified, but by the One in whose hands Muḥammad's life reposes, the sanctity and honour of a believer, his life and his property, is far greater than yours in the eyes of God.[11]

ما أطيبك وما أطيب ريحك، وما أعظمك وما أعظم حرمتك، والذى نفس محمد بيده لحرمة المؤمن عند اللّه أعظم من حرمتك ماله ودمه.

These clear affirmations of the dignity of man are in turn endorsed in a variety of other contexts in the Qur'ān and *Sunnah*, one of which is the basic unity in the creation of mankind, and its equality in the eyes of the Creator.

NOTES

1. Maḥmūd al-Alūsī, *Rūḥ al-Maʿānī fī Tafsīr al-Qur'ān al-ʿAẓīm*, Beirut, Dār al-Turāth al-ʿArabī, n.d., vol. XV, p. 117.
2. Muṣṭafā al-Sibāʿī, *Ishtirākiyyāt al-Islām*, 2nd edn, Damascus, al-Dār al-Qawmiyyah li'l-Ṭibaʿah wa'l-Nashr, 1379/1960, p. 66; ʿAbd al-Ḥakīm Ḥasan

al-ʿĪlī, *al-Ḥurriyyāt al-ʿĀmmah*, Cairo, Dār al-Fikr, 1403/1983, p. 361.

3. Aḥmad Yusrī, *Ḥuqūq al-Insān wa Asbāb al-ʿUnf fi'l-Mujtamaʿ al-Islāmī fī Ḍaw' Aḥkām al-Sharīʿah*, Alexandria (Egypt), Mansha'at al-Maʿārif, 1993, p. 30.

4. Sayyid Quṭb, *al-ʿAdālah al-Ijtimāʿiyyah fi'l-Islām*, 4th edn, Cairo, ʿIsā al-Bābī al-Ḥalabī, 1373/1954, p. 59.

5. Wahbah al-Zuḥaylī, *al-Fiqh al-Islāmī wa Adillatuh*, 3rd edn, 8 vols., Damascus, Dār al-Fikr, 1409/1989, VI, 720.

6. Quṭb, *al-ʿAdālah al-Ijtimāʿiyyah* p. 30; al-ʿĪlī, *Ḥurriyyāt*, p. 361; Muḥammad Abū Zahrah, *Tanẓīm al-Islām li'l-Mujtamaʿ*, Cairo, Dār al-Fikr al-ʿArabī, 1385/1965, p. 28.

7. Muḥammad al-Ghazālī, *Ḥuqūq al-Insān bayn Taʿālīm al-Islām wa Iʿlān al-Umam al-Muttaḥidah*, Alexandria (Egypt), Dār al-Daʿwah li'l-Nashr wa'l-Tawziʿ, 1413/1993, p. 37. The reference to Ibn Ḥazm is to his *al-Muḥallā* (*K. al-Janā'iz*) where similar other reports concerning the Companions have also been recorded.

8. Ibid.

9. J. Weeramantry, *Islamic Jurisprudence: An International Perspective*, Basingstoke (UK), Macmillan, 1988, p. 64.

10. ʿAbd Allāh al-Khaṭīb al-Tabrīzī, *Mishkāt al-Maṣabīḥ*, ed. Muḥammad Nāṣir al-Dīn al-Albānī, 2nd edn, Beirut, al-Maktab al-Islāmī, 1399/1979, vol. II, *ḥadīth* no. 4998.

11. Al-Tabrīzī, *Mishkāt*, vol. II, *ḥadīth* no. 2724.

CHAPTER TWO

Fraternity of Man

The Qur'ānic vision of mankind is basically that of a single, unified entity, regardless of any differences of origin and status. Unity and equality are the necessary postulates of human dignity, as without these human dignity as a universal value will necessarily be compromised. One of the most explicit passages in the Qur'ān on the unity inherent in the essence and origin of mankind is as follows:

> O mankind! Keep your duty to your Lord, who created you from a single soul and created its mate of the same [kind] and created from them countless men and women. And keep your duty to your Lord, by Whom you demand your rights from one another, and [observe] the ties of kinship. (al-Nisā', 4:1)

يا أيها الناس أتقو ربكم الذى خلقكم من نفس واحدة وخلق منها زوجها وبث منهما رجالاً كثيراً ونساءا واتقوا اللّه الذى تساءلون به والأرحام.

The key phrase in this text is '*khalaqakum min nafsin wāḥidatin*'—'He created you from a single soul'—which also occurs in identical terms elsewhere in the Qur'ān (al-Zumar, 39:6). This phrase seems to imply, in addition to its immediate meaning, that Eve was not created, as it were, from Adam's rib, but made in a like manner, and God breathed into them both of His own spirit. What is in common is this soul, and this is confirmed by the fact that in both *āyāt*, the reference to it is in the female singular (i.e. *minhā*), which could not be a reference to Adam. The Prophet ﷺ has added his voice to this message of unity in the following *ḥadīth*: 'O people, your Creator is one; you are all from the same ancestor; all of you are from Adam, and Adam was created from earth.'[1]

يا أيها الناس إنّ ربكم واحد وإن أباكم واحد، كلّكم لآدم وآدم من تراب.

The Qur'ān provides evidence to the effect that Islam validates and combines in its own teachings the basic values of other revealed religions. As such, Islam is addressed to humanity at large, and all its basic teachings on justice, promotion of good and prevention of evil (*amr bi'l-maʿrūf wa nahy ʿan al-munkar*), the doing of good (*iḥsān*), co-operation in good works (*taʿāwun*) and building and beautifying the earth (*ʿimār al-arḍ*) are addressed to all people. Similarly, the Qur'ānic designation of *khilāfah*, that is, God's appointment of man as His vicegerent on earth, and the numerous references in the Qur'ān to the subjugation (*taskhīr*) of the universe to the benefit of man, are addressed to the whole of mankind. The essence of worship (*ʿibādah*) is also a common theme of all religions, as the Qur'ān declares in its address:

> O mankind! Worship your Lord who created you and those who came before you so that you attain excellence of conduct. (al-Baqarah, 2: 21)

ياايّها النّاس اعبدوا ربّكم الّذى خلقكم والّذين من قبلكم لعلّكم تتّقون.

The Qur'ān is also addressed to humanity at large, as indicated in the following *āyah*:

> O mankind! A proof has come to you from your Lord in which there is clear enlightenment for you. (al-Nisā' 4:174)

يا ايّها النّاس قد جاء كم برهان من ربّكم وانزلنا اليكم نورا مبينا.

The substance of this last *āyah* is upheld elsewhere, where the Qur'ān refers to itself by saying:

This is an explanation for mankind, guidance and good advice to the God-fearing. (Āl ʿImrān, 3:138)

هذا بيان للنّاس وهدى وموعظة للمتّقين.

Yet another Qur'ānic address provides:

O mankind! There has come to you an exhortation from your Lord, a healing for [spiritual ailments] in your hearts, and guidance and mercy for the believers. (Yūnus, 10:57)

يا ايّها النّاس قد جاء تكم موعظة من ربّكم وشفاء لما في الصدور وهدى ورحمة للمؤمنين.

The typical Qur'ānic address 'O people' (*yā ayyuhā al-nās*) is 'for humanity at large without any specification of a section or group thereof. All are therefore included without any exception whatsoever'.[2] Whereas some previous scriptures and prophets were, by their own acknowledgement, sent and addressed to particular groups of people, such the prophet Lot, for example, the prophethood of Muḥammad ﷺ was not so confined—as God Most High addressed Muḥammad ﷺ in the Qur'ān:

And We have not sent you but as a warner and bringer of good news to all people. (Saba', 34:28)

وما أرسلناك إلا كآفّة للنّاس بشيرا ونذيرا

Unity in origin, unity in creation, and unity in basic values necessarily means that Islam seeks to bring benefit and improvement to all people and all races. They must all enjoy equality and equal treatment without any discrimination. Abū Zahrah has to this effect quoted a *ḥadīth* wherein the Prophet ﷺ said that 'God does not look at your faces but He looks at your hearts'.[3]

انّ اللّه لاينظر الى صوركم ولكن ينظر الى قلوبكم.

Thus intentions and one's actions are more important than who one is. Abū Zahrah has also recorded an incident in which the Prophet ﷺ heard a man calling another 'Ibn al-Sawdā' (the son of a black woman) and then emphatically said:

> The measure has been exceeded, the measure has been exceeded, the measure has been exceeded. The son of a white woman has no superiority over the son of a black woman except on grounds of God–consciousness.

لقد طفّ الكيل، لقد طفّ الكيل، لقد طفّ الكيل، ليس لابن البيضاء على ابن السوداء فضل إلا بالتقوى

Since all people are brothers and sisters and all being the children of Adam, 'there could be no affront to the human dignity of any single person without there being an affront to the dignity of all—including the dignity of the perpetrator of the indignity'.[4] In making this observation, Weeramantry elaborates that man, being God's prize creation on whom 'He had showered His choicest blessings, could not be subject to a violation of that dignity by man'.[5]

It is a basic right of all human being to live a life of dignity, complemented by peace and comfort and the freedom to pursue what brings them happiness and perfection through all lawful means.[6] A Muslim only worships God as his sole Creator and Sovereign and humbles himself to no one else. The creation and enjoyment of beauty, good health and a clean environment are seen as complementary to the dignified lifestyle of Islam. The Prophet thus said in a *ḥadīth*: 'God is beautiful and loves beauty', just as we read in another *ḥadīth* that 'cleanliness is a part of faith'.

انّ اللّه جميل وهو يحبّ الجمال.

الطهور شطر الايمان.

NOTES

1. From the Sermon on the occasion of Farewell Pilgrimage (*Ḥajjat al-Widāᶜ*). See Aḥmad Ibn ᶜAbd Rabbih, *al-ᶜIqd al-Farīd li'l-Malik al-Saᶜīd*, 3rd edn, 15 vols., Cairo, Maṭbaᶜat Lajnat al-Ta'lif, 1384/1965; II, 35; Ṣubḥī Mahmaṣṣānī, *Arkān Ḥuqūq al-Insān fi'l-Islām*, Beirut, Dār al-ᶜIlm li'l-Malāyīn, 1979, p. 266.

2. Muḥammad Abū Zahrah, *al-Mujtamaᶜ al-Insānī fī Ẓill al-Islām*, 2nd edn, Jeddah, Dār al-Ṣuᶜūdiyyah, 1401/1981, p. 48.

3. Ibid., pp. 50-1.

4. Weeramantry, *Islamic Jurisprudence*, p. 64.

5. Ibid.

6. Cf. Wahbah al-Zuḥaylī, *Ḥaqq al-Ḥurriyyah fi'l-ᶜĀlam*, Beirut, Dār al-Fikr al-Muᶜāṣir, 1417/1997, pp. 93-4.

CHAPTER THREE

Man's Physical and Spiritual Pre-eminence

With regard to the creation and physical image of man, the Qur'ān refers in the first place to God's omnipotence and unqualified power of choice in creating man in any image that pleases Him: 'In whatever form He wills, He puts you together' (al-Infiṭār, 82:8).

فى أ ى صورة ما شاء ركّبك.

It is then declared: 'Indeed, We created man in the best of forms' (al-Tīn, 95:4)

لقد خلقنا الانسان في أحسن تقويم.

and then again: 'He fashioned you in the best of images' (al-Mu'min, 40:64; al-Taghābun, 64:3).

وصّوركم فأحسن صوركم.

The physical attributes of beauty and elegance in the creation of man are then matched by a spiritual endowment of the highest order, whereby God Most High declares that 'I breathed into him [Adam] of My spirit' (Ṣād, 38:72).

ونفخت فيه من روحى.

There is also evidence in the Qur'ān of direct divine involvement, or a level of intimacy, so to speak, in man's creation, which is indicative of God's love for human beings. This can be seen in a context, as quoted below, that is initially expressive of God's displeasure with Satan for his refusal to prostrate to Adam, as he was asked to do, and then refers to the manner in which God created man:

> [God] said: O Iblīs, what prevents thee from prostrating thyself to one whom I have created with My hands? (Ṣād, 38:75)

قال يا إبليس ما منعك أن تسجد لما خلقت بيدى.

This divine involvement in man's creation was what Satan had ignored in his initial response that 'you created him [Adam] from clay and created me from fire' (Ṣād, 38:76).

خلقتنى من نار و خلقته من طين.

But in saying this, Satan ignored the fact that Adam was God's prize creation and partook of the spirit of God. Then God asked the angels to prostrate before Adam, which they duly did, and this established the spiritual superiority of Adam over the angels. The text thus declares:

> We created you and moulded you in shape. Then We told the angels to prostrate to Adam, and they prostrated; not so Iblīs. He refused to be of those who prostrate. (al-Aʿrāf, 7:11)

ولقد خلقناكم ثم صوّرناكم ثم قلنا للملائكة اسجدوا لآدم
فسجدوا إلا إبليس لم يكن من الساجدين.

Another related aspect of the dignified image of man in the eyes of his Creator is his appointment as God's vicegerent (*khalīfah*) on the earth and the bearer of His trust. Man's mission as *khalīfah* on the earth is to build the earth, and to establish a just order therein in accordance with God's will and His *Sharīʿah*. God thus revealed His purpose to the angels, saying that 'I am appointing a vicegerent (*khalīfah*) on the earth'. The angels demurred with awe but protested that they should have been entrusted with this honour: 'We praise and glorify thee', whereas man is prone to corruption and violence. Then the angels were told: 'I know what you know not.' The text continues to declare that 'God taught Adam the names of things' and thus confirms his superior capacity for knowledge and reason than that of the angels'. The angels then acceded to Adam's suitability for the assignment of *khilāfah* and said, 'Praise be to Thee; we do not know except for what You taught us. You are the All-knowing, All-wise.' (al-Baqarah, 2:30-32)

إني جاعل في الأرض خليفةً [...] ونحن نسبح بحمدك ونقدس لك [...] إنى أعلم ما لا تعلمون. وعلم آدم الأسماء كلها [...] قالوا سبحنك لا علم لنا إلا ما علمتنا إنك أنت العليم الحكيم.

God's decision to make mankind the repository of prophethood and the principal audience and recipient of His final message, that is, the Qur'ān, further testifies to the trust with which God has honoured mankind.

CHAPTER FOUR

God's Love for Humanity

The Qur'ān confirms that man's creation was a unique act of creation. It was distinguished from God's creation of the rest of the heavens and the earth in that these were created by God's will and command, whereas man's creation was an expression of divine love. This is manifested, as the Qur'ān confirms, in God's direct involvement in the creation of man. Man is depicted as God's handiwork, whom He designed in the best image and form, and then breathed into him of His own spirit. God's love for mankind is also manifested in His command to the angels, and Satan, to prostrate themselves before Adam. Prostration is a supreme act of humility and devotion, something that God would normally reserve for Himself. God's direct involvement also signifies the intimacy and closeness of the God-man relationship, which did not cease with the first act of creation but continues to be expressed and unfolded as a reality through the religious experiences of the believers.

Since religion is the matrix of the God-man relationship, it is founded, in the case of Islam, on divine love, mercy and grace. The rituals of the faith, the prayer and supplication, when engaged in with sincerity, are expressive of man's devotion to and love for God, which is, as God taught His beloved servants to feel, without intermediaries. This is witnessed by the fact that Islam does not have a church or a clergy that mediates between God and man, and no one exercises spiritual mediation of any kind in Islam. A Muslim relates directly to his Creator, at any time and in any place. God made His unceasing interest in and involvement with man's affairs known when He declared in the Qur'ān: 'Wherever you turn, there is the Face of God' (al-Baqarah, 2:115).

فأينما تولوا فثم وجه الله.

Elsewhere it is stated in an address to the Prophet ﷺ: 'When My servants ask you concerning Me, I am indeed close to them. I listen to the prayer of every supplicant when he calls on Me' (al-Baqarah, 2:186).

واذا سألك عبادى عنى فإني قريب أجيب دعوة الدّاع اذا دعان.

Since man is created in God's image, he is endowed with the appropriate faculties to perfect himself and fulfil his enormous potential. This is noted in what the Qur'ān singles out as one of the most distinctive of God's favours on mankind. The Qur'ānic sūra al-Raḥmān (the Compassionate) thus begins with these words:

> God the Most Compassionate! It is He who taught the Qur'ān; He who created man and taught him speech. (al-Raḥmān, 55:1-4)

الرحمن علم القرآن خلق الإنسان علّمه البيان.

It was, in other words, a manifestation of God's love and grace that He revealed the Qur'ān and endowed man with the capacity for speech. God Most High communicated with man through the Qur'ān, and then enabled man, by His grace, to communicate through language. The Qur'ān thus designates itself the carrier of God's message of love and beneficence, which is manifested in the endowment of man with the faculty of speech.

This feature of the Qur'ān, that is, the manifestation of God's love for humanity, has found more explicit expression in Sufi thought and understanding of Islam than it has in juristic expositions. Be that as it may, there is direct evidence in the Qur'ān of the love of God (*ḥubb Allāh*) for those who believe in Him and do not associate any other with his divinity. God has demanded sincere devotion from man, which is expressed by worshipping Him. Man has consequently been exhorted thus:

> So remember Me and I will remember you. Be grateful to me and reject Me not. O you who believe, seek My help with patience and with prayer. (al-Baqarah, 2:152-153)

فاذكروني أذكركم واشكروا لي ولا تكفرون. يا أيها الذين آمنوا استعينوا بالصبر والصّلاة.

The *āyāt* preceding this one in the same sūra also speak of worship and devotion to God, and then of God's reassurance to man:

> So that I may complete My favours on you and you may be guided. (al-Baqarah, 2:150)

ولأتّم نعمتي عليكم لعلكم تهتدون.

The Qur'ān also contains direct references to the believers' love for God in contradistinction with those who associate others with His divinity. Note the following passage for example:

> And your Lord is one; there is no God but He, Most Compassionate, Most Merciful [...] Yet there are men who take [for worship] others besides God as equals with Him. They love them as they should love God. But those who have faith are overflowing in their love for God. (al-Baqarah, 2:163-165)

وإلهكم إله واحد لا إله إلا هو الرّحمن الرّحيم [...] ومن الناس من يتخذ من دون اللّه أنداداً يحبونهم كحب اللّه والذين آمنوا أشدّ حباً للّه.

God's love is enhanced for those who adhere to His message, His Messenger ﷺ and His guidance. The Prophet ﷺ thus declares to his followers: 'If you do love God, follow me, God will love you and forgive your failings' (Āl ʿImrān, 3:31).

إن كنتم تحبون اللّه فاتبعوني يحببكم اللّه ويغفر لكم ذنوبكم.

Forgiveness emanates from love and God promises that He 'forgives all sins except association of other [deities] with Him' (al-Nisā', 4:48).

إن اللّه لا يغفر أن يشرك به ويغفر ما دون ذلك لمن يشاء.

This is the breaking point at which a man's love for God no longer exists, that is, when he considers other deities worthy of worship.

Sincerity in giving charity for the love of God above and beyond conformity to rituals is emphasised in the Qur'ān where it states: 'It is not a virtue to turn your faces [in prayer] to the East and the West, but virtue is to have faith [...] and spend of your wealth out of love for Him' (al-Baqarah, 2:177).

ليس البّر أن تولّوا وجوهكم قبل المشرق والمغرب ولكن البرّ من آمن باللّه [...] وآتي المال على حبه ذوي القربى.

The Qur'ān has in many places spelt out the ways and means by which man can earn God's love. These are all meant to serve as incentives to virtuous conduct. God's love is undoubtedly earned through virtuous conduct. But sincerity and devotion enhance the value of that conduct. Love and devotion are the building blocks of the God-man relationship. Faith is not a formality nor conformity to rituals by any means, notwithstanding the persuasive language of the jurists which has almost managed to constrict the emotional appeal of the Qur'ān by means of a plethora of legal rules. To argue that love and devotion are not a matter of conformity to rules is evident in the emotionally-anchored language of the Qur'ānic address. A perusal of the Qur'ān thus leaves little doubt that Islam is faith and devotion in the first place, and legal rules and rituals second. Also, God's love is tied up with the love of His beloved servants. Note for example: 'God truly loves those who are conscious of Him' (al-Tawbah, 9:4 and 9:7)

إن اللّه يحب المتقين.

and 'God loves those who are good to others' (al-Baqarah, 2:195)

واحسنوا إن اللّه يحب المحسنين.

and 'God loves those who place their trust in Him' (Āl ʿImrān, 3:159)

إن اللّه يحب المتوكلين.

The Qur'ān continuously lists God's promises of love for those who love other human beings, who remain patient in the face of adversity (*al-ṣābirīn*), those who are fair to others (*al-muqsiṭīn*), those who repent and ask for forgiveness (*al-tawwābīn*), those who are pure and observant of cleanliness (*al-mutaṭahhirīn*), (Āl ʿImrān, 3:146; al-Mā'idah, 5:42; al-Baqarah, 2:222) and so on. Patience in the face of adversity could be for various motives but the most meritorious are 'those who patiently persevere while seeking the countenance of their Lord' (al-Raʿd, 13:22). The expression *wajh Allāh* (lit. the face of God), which signifies intimacy and love, occurs in many places in the Qur'ān, especially in reference to those who give generously to the poor 'seeking the countenance of God' (cf. Al-Rūm, 30:38 and 39) and 'have nothing in their minds [...] but only the desire to seek for the countenance of their Lord Most High' (al-Layl, 92:19-20).

وما لأحد عنده من نعمة تجزى إلا ابتغاء وجه ربه الأعلى.

In an unusually candid style, God has elsewhere addressed His beloved prophet Moses in these terms: 'And I cast My love over you in order that you may be reared under My eye' (Ṭā Ḥā, 20:39).

وألقيت عليك محبة مني ولتصنع على عيني.

Notwithstanding the demands that are attached to earning God's love, His unbounded mercy and love extend even to those who fall into error and sin, as the Qur'ān confirms:

> O my servants who have transgressed against their souls! Do not despair of the mercy of God. For God forgives all sins. He is most forgiving, most merciful. (al-Zumar, 39:53)

قل ياعبادي الذين أسرفوا على أنفسهم لا تقنطوا من رحمة اللّه إن اللّه يغفر الذنوب جميعا إنه هو الغفور الرحيم.

Despair and disappointment are the opposite of love, as one who despairs is convinced of the absence of love. This is what the Qur'ān conveys even more emphatically when it declares: 'And who else but the misguided would despair of the mercy of his Lord?' (al-Ḥijr, 15:56)

ومن يقنط من رحمة ربّه إلا الضالّون.

The following statement is also nothing less than an open declaration of God's love: 'My mercy engulfs everything and extends beyond everything' (al-Aʿrāf, 7:156).

ورحمتي وسعت كل شئ.

The focus is nevertheless on human beings. Thus it is declared in a *ḥadīth* that, 'One who does not show compassion to the people, God will not be compassionate toward him.'[1]

لا يرحم اللّه من لا يرحم الناس.

It is also interesting to note that of the ninety-nine Most Beautiful Names of God (*al-asmā' al-ḥusnā*), the two most favoured by God Himself are 'al-Raḥmān' and 'al-Raḥīm'—the Beneficent, the Merciful. For only these are chosen to appear at the beginning of every chapter of the Qur'ān. Ibn ʿĀbidīn has interestingly observed that while al-Raḥīm is meant for the believers, al-Raḥmān extends to everyone, believers and non-believers alike.[2] God's Most Beautiful Names also include 'al-Ḥabīb' (the Loving), 'al-Laṭīf' (Most Gracious) and 'al-Wadūd' (Most Affectionate).

God's love of man, His mercy and compassion are meant for mankind as a whole without any qualification, and encompasses people of all faiths, and those who may not even subscribe to any religion. For God's love, like all His other attributes, is absolute. If God's love was the cause of man's creation, then, like His bestowal of the attribute of dignity upon man, His love too is unqualified and all-encompassing.[3] So is God's mercy, which is boundless and does not just extend to individuals and groups of individuals, but to the whole of mankind and even more. It is neither conditional nor anticipatory of gratitude and recognition. For God Most High praises, as noted above, those who show generosity to the poor for the sake of

God alone, without expecting reciprocity or gratitude.[4] If God admires unconditional giving in His servants, would He Himself choose to act in any other way? This point is expressive of an aspect of God's own attribute, which amounts to perfection in every respect. When love is made conditional, it surely loses its purity and perfection. 'God's love is proven [and meant to be] for all people regardless of religion. For love is the cause of man's creation, which is why no one can be excluded. The same is true of God's conferment of dignity on the progeny of Adam.'[5]

What is said here, however, is not to deny the greater reward that individuals may expect for meritorious conduct. When it is stated, in so many places in the Qur'ān, that God loves those who are assiduous in pursuit of good work, perseverant, pure and the like, these are indicative of grades of distinction and reward. Similarly, the universal Qur'ānic declaration on the dignity of man is not compromised by its other declaration that 'the most noble among you before God is the one who excels in God-consciousness' (al-Ḥujurāt, 49:13).

إن أكرمكم عند الله أتقاكم.

The vivid affirmation of God's love and compassion for man in the Qur'ān sets the basic framework for relationships among human beings themselves. God's love of man must surely be emulated by men in regard to each other. One commentator has put this more forcefully in saying that, 'since God Most High has taken it upon Himself to respect the dignity of mankind, the latter is surely under a duty to observe the same among its members, to preserve its own integrity and avoid its violation'.[6] The Qur'ānic declaration that 'verily the believers are brethren' (al-Ḥujurāt, 49:10)

إنما المؤمنون اخوة.

is endorsed in an almost identical declaration by the Prophet ﷺ, who said: 'The believer is the brother of the believer.'[7] In yet another *ḥadīth* the Prophet ﷺ declared, 'None of you is a [true] believer unless he loves for his brother what he loves for himself.'[8]

لا يؤمن أحدكم حتى يحب لأخيه ما يحب لنفسه.

Love, dignity and compassion thus constitute the basic ingredients of the relationship that the believers must nurture among themselves.

I conclude this discussion with a Qur'ānic *āyah* which declares in totally emphatic and unqualified terms that 'God is truly compassionate and merciful to mankind' (al-Ḥajj, 22:65).

إن الله بالناس لرؤف رحيم

NOTES

1. Al-Tabrīzī, *Mishkāt*, vol. III, *ḥadīth* no. 4678.
2. Muḥammad Amīn ibn ʿĀbidīn, *Hāshiyah Radd al-Mukhtār ʿalā Durr al-Mukhtār*, 2nd edn, Cairo, Muṣṭafā al-Bābi al-Ḥalabī, 1386/1966, I, 6; Yusrī, *Ḥuqūq al-Insān*, p. 35.
3. Yusrī, *Ḥuqūq al-Insān*, p. 33.
4. Those who give to others and say, 'We feed you for God's pleasure only; we desire from you neither reward nor gratitude' (al-Insān, 76:9). See also al-Layl, 92:20 to similar effect.
5. Yusrī, *Ḥuqūq al-Insān*, p. 33.
6. Ibid., pp. 31-32.
7. Al-Tabrīzī, *Mishkāt*, vol. III, *ḥadīth* no. 4958.
8. Muḥyī al-Dīn al-Nawawī, *Riyāḍ al-Ṣāliḥīn*, ed. Muḥammad Nāṣir al-Dīn al-Albānī, 2nd edn, Beirut, Dār al-Maktab al-Islāmī, 1404/1984, p. 113, *ḥadīth* no. 118.

CHAPTER FIVE

Right to Personal Safety

It is a manifestation of the dignity of man that Islam has placed an infinite value on human life. This is expressed in the Qur'ān in the following terms:

> We ordained for the children of Israel that if anyone slew a person, unless it was for murder or for spreading mischief in the land, it would be as if he slew the whole of mankind. And if anyone saved a life, it would be as if he saved the whole of mankind. (al-Mā'idah, 5:32)

وكتبنا على بنى إسرائيل أنه من قتل نفسا بغير نفس أو فساد في الأرض فكأنما قتل الناس جميعاً. ومن أحياها فكأنما أحيا الناس جميعاً.

The reference to the children of Israel, that is, the Jews, represents the continuity of the basic values that are common to all revealed religions. Both Judaism and Islam are committed to the protection of human life. It makes no difference whether the victim is a Jew, a Muslim or anyone else. The value that is advocated is holistic and indivisible in that aggression against one is tantamount to aggression against all. Life is not only of infinite value, it is also sacred: 'Nor take life, which God has made sacred, except for a just cause' (al-Isrā', 17:33).

ولا تقتلوا النفس التى حرم اللّه إلا بالحق.

Al-Ghazālī has quoted these *āyāt* and draws the conclusion that 'in respect of the sanctity of life and the prohibition of aggression against it, Muslims and non-Muslims are equal. An attack on the personal safety of non-Muslims invokes the same punishment in this world and the Hereafter'.[1]

In times of military engagement, combatants have a personal responsibility not to destroy civilian life. It is consequently unlawful to attack women and children, the elderly and the insane, the ill and the invalids (and this include the blind, the lame, the crippled and the unconscious). The exempted categories also include the priest and the monk and those engaged in worship, as well as farmers who occupy themselves with their works in the field provided that they are not involved in the conflict. The *ḥadīth* contains detailed instructions on all of these and the Prophet ﷺ has generally advised military commanders and soldiers on the battlefield to be fair, avoid excessive violence and to be incline towards peace.[2]

It is a collective duty (*farḍ kifā'ī*) of the community to ensure the safety of an abandoned infant (*al-laqīṭ*) found on the street, and this responsibility becomes the personal duty (*farḍ ᶜayn*) of the person who may alone be in a position to save the infant's life. Those who are, in fact, able to save the *laqīṭ* but fail to do so, incur a sin and are accountable for this. It is then the duty of the government to take care of the infant, its upbringing and education. The state's responsibility for the welfare of unclaimed infants is even more emphatic than that for children who live with their parents, simply because the head of state becomes the guardian (*walī*) of children who have no father or guardian. The second caliph, ᶜUmar ibn al-Khaṭṭāb used to allocate a monthly sum of one hundred dirhams and food supplements for the *laqīṭ*, which was reviewed annually and increased in accordance with age. He paid this out of the funds of the public treasury and used to remind the people to be good and generous to such children.[3]

Since saving the abandoned infant (*iltiqāṭ*) is a *Sharīᶜah* obligation, it is a violation of that duty for anyone to discard a baby, initially or at any stage, before or after it is picked up and found. The life of that infant is absolutely sacrosanct and no excuse can justify its exposure to destruction and danger.[4] The jurists have also held that exposing an infant to danger is forbidden even if it is done with the approval and agreement of the parents. Parental agreement in this case is of no value and will carry no credibility at all.[5] Priority is also given, in judicial decisions concerning children, to the best interest of the children, the realisation of their material and moral needs, and the protection of their basic human dignity. According to the rules of *fiqh,* when a divorced woman with a child remarries, the right of custody (*ḥaḍānah*) transfers to the father, but the judge may give it back to the mother, or any other relative who is deemed best suited to look after the welfare of the child.[6]

Since life is a God-given gift and only God creates it, no one has the authority to destroy it without just cause. This also applies to homicide, which is an offence under the *Sharīʿah* for which the perpetrator is accountable to God and liable to a deterrent sanctioned by the court in the event of an unsuccessful attempt. If the attempt succeeds, the person is still liable to expiation (*kaffārah*), which may be taken from his property, according to the Shāfiʿīs and some Ḥanbalīs, whereas the Imāms Mālik and Abū Ḥanīfah do not make *kaffārah* a requirement.[7]

The Qur'ānic authority on the prohibition of suicide is found in its unequivocal directive 'kill not yourselves, for God is merciful to you' (al-Nisā', 4:29). God Most High also gives cause for hope to those of His Servants who might have been overwhelmed by despair and might have considered suicide as a way out of their predicament:

> O my servants who have indulged into excess concerning themselves! Despair not of the mercy of God. For God forgives all sins. (al-Zumār, 39:53)

يا عبادي الّذين أسرفوا على انفسهم لاتقنطوا من رحمة اللّه، انّ اللّه يغفر الذنوب جميعا.

The substance of these declarations is confirmed in another Qur'ānic text where not only suicide but also virtually any attempt, whether direct or indirect, to endanger life has been proscribed:

> And throw not yourselves into [the mouth of] perdition by your own hands. (al-Baqarah, 2:195)

ولا تلقوا بأيديكم إلى التهلكة

The directive here includes all life-threatening situations that can be avoided through caution: taking up dangerous assignments, consuming dangerous drugs and courting lethal and insidious diseases such as AIDS. Furthermore, on the subject of suicide, it is provided in a *ḥadīth* that:

> One who throws himself off a mountain cliff and kills himself as a result will be doing the same permanently to himself in Hell. And one who takes poison and kills himself as a result shall be holding the same poison in his hand taking it permanently in Hell.[8]

Life, in the terminology of *Sharīᶜah*, is a trust (*amānah*) on the shoulders of its bearer, and carries with it a responsibility for its protection against danger and abuse. Life is also seen as a testing ground for everyone, especially those who undergo hardship and pain, and for them, as indeed for all mortals, the advice is to seek God's help by turning to Him in supplication and hope while remaining patient and perseverant in the face of adversity.

A person's agreement with or permission to another to kill or destroy him is of no value in the *Sharīᶜah*, and if this carried out, the perpetrator is liable to retaliation and punishment. This is because the bearer of life is not his own originator and therefore has no authority to validate its destruction.[9]

The *Sharīᶜah* also grants many concessions to individuals to enable them to protect themselves against threats to security or health. With regard to religious duties, such as the daily prayers and the ritual ablutions that precede it, a man who may be unable, due to danger, injury or disease, to use water for ablution, may instead perform a dry ablution with clean sand (*tayammum*) for prayer. *Tayammum* is also valid for an individual who may be anxious to save drinking water that may be in short supply, not only for himself but also to quench the thirst of a thirsty animal. For reasons of safety, it is also permissible to face a different direction than that of the *qiblah* and perform prayer, if one has to. The ritual prayer that involves bodily movement may also be shortened or performed in a different and easier posture that may avoid moving a painful organ. This is in compliance with the general *Sharīᶜah* rule on the avoidance of hardship. A sick and elderly person and a pregnant woman are likewise not required to fast during the fasting month of Ramaḍān. It is also permissible for a person to disrupt his prayer and avert danger from an oncoming animal or object and then return to complete the rest of his prayer from where he left it. The intervening activity neither disrupts nor vitiates the *ṣalāh*. Similarly, it is obligatory on the individual, man or woman, who hears the cries of a drowning person, or one who faces imminent death, to disrupt his prayer and rush to help him if he or she can. To alert a blind man or child to the danger of falling into a pit is not only permissible during prayer but is a requirement under the *Sharīʿah*, which means that prayer must be disrupted in order to avert danger to a human being.

In the event where performing the normal *ḥajj* ceremonies prove hazardous to heath due, for example, to exposure to the sun, or if wearing the seamless white garment of *iḥrām* needs to be avoided, the necessary adjustment may be made by following correct medical advice, even if this means changing parts of the ritual performances of the *ḥajj*.

In the event where eating unlawful substances, such as pork, carcasses and alcohol, which are normally forbidden, would mean facing death by starvation or thirst, the *Sharīʿah* allows them to be consumed on grounds of necessity (*ḍarūrah*). Drinking alcohol is forbidden, but if a person chokes while eating and no liquid other than wine is available, he may consume it to the extent necessary to avert danger.

Marriage is a firm covenant and a life-long union in Islam, and divorce is, according to a renowned *ḥadīth*, 'the worst of all permissible things in the sight of God'. Yet if one spouse is afflicted with an illness that makes life difficult for the other, the *Sharīʿah* allows the latter to seek judicial annulment of the marriage. The Prophet ﷺ also advised that a pregnant woman should not suckle a baby, as it is likely that breast-feeding at that time weakens the suckling child and also affects the healthy growth of the foetus. The pregnant woman is further advised not to exert herself in hard work, during the advanced stages of pregnancy, on a temporary basis at least. Pregnancy is strongly discouraged, on the other hand, in the event where an illness of one or both the parents is likely to affect the normal growth of the offspring.

Mutilation of human body parts is normally forbidden, but is permitted on medical grounds if it will save life. Similarly, the law forbids taking another person's property without his consent, but permits a starving person to rob another of his excess food or water if this will save his life, in the event where the owner refuses to give them freely. Muslims are also required to respect the Qur'ān and also books and papers which carry God's illustrious name, but if it proves necessary to step on these and place them under one's feet in order to obtain water or food at a height that cannot be otherwise reached, all of these are permissible if they will save life.

The Prophet ﷺ frequently gave advice to fight illness and disease through recourse to medical treatment and refused to succumb to fatalism. According to the Prophet's instruction, if one hears of the outbreak of contageous disease in a district or region, one should not go there, but if one is already in that place, one should not travel or take the disease to other places. The Prophet ﷺ has also said in another *ḥadīth* that a Muslim who is healthy and strong is a better Muslim than one who is afflicted, slovenly and weak.[10]

Furthermore, the *Sharīᶜah* forbids abortion after the inception of the life of the foetus. Abortion after the inception of life (i.e. *nafkh al-rūḥ*) is held to be *ḥarām* and equivalent to a crime committed on a living person. The law makes the aggressor liable to the payment of blood money (*diyyah*) if the foetus emerges alive and then dies, and of a *ghurrah* (that is half of a full *diyyah*), if the foetus emerges dead. *Diyyah* and *ghurrah* under these circumstances are payable to the mother.[11]

Abortion prior to the inception of life in the womb has provoked different responses from the *ᶜulamā'*. The Shāfiᶜīs have allowed it during the first forty days of pregnancy provided that the spouses are in agreement on the issue and it is not harmful to the mother. Abortion is forbidden after forty days, which is believed to be the starting point of life. Abortion is only permitted at this stage if it will help save the life of the mother.

In the event of the death of a pregnant woman, the law permits incision and cutting open her womb in order to save a child that is known to be still alive.

Breast-feeding is a right of the child over the mother who is capable and fit, and the mother must give her own child priority over others whom she may be breast-feeding for reasons of earning money or the like.

With regard to the basic interests of children, the Prophet ﷺ has singled out education saying that 'a father gives his son nothing better than a good education'.[12] In another *ḥadīth*, the Prophet ﷺ said that, 'He who is not kind to [our] children is not one of us.'[13]

ليس منا من لا يرحم صغيرنا.

In yet another *ḥadīth*, the Prophet ﷺ spoke of the merit gained by the care and protection of orphans and said: 'I and the person who looks after an orphan and provides for him will be in Paradise like this', putting his index and middle fingers together.[14]

أنا وكافل اليتيم في الجنة هكذا وقال بإصبعيه السبابة والوسطى.

The Qur'ān is emphatic in its demand for the fair treatment of orphans. This is, in fact, one of its recurrent themes, referred to in numerous places. In one of these passages the Qur'ān warns that 'those who wrongfully devour the property of orphans truly swallow fire into their bellies' (al-Nisā', 4:10).

إن الذين يأكلون أموال اليتامى ظلماً إنما يأكلون في بطونهم نارا.

This verse made some people, who were taking care of orphans, anxious about the consequences of some unintentional miscalculation or incidental mishandling on their part, and asked the Prophet ﷺ about this. Thus another Qur'ānic *āyah* reads:

> They ask you about the orphans. Say: to set right their affairs should be the purpose, but if you mix their property with yours [or become partners with them], they are your brethren. And God knows the one who makes mischief from the one who means well' (al-Baqarah, 2:220).

ويسألونك عن اليتامى قل اصلاح لهم خير وإن تخالطوهم فإخوانكم والله يعلم المفسد من المصلح.

Elsewhere the Qur'ān addresses the Prophet ﷺ in these words: 'Treat not the orphan with harshness.' (al-Ḍuḥā, 93:9)

فأما اليتيم فلا تقهر.

In another place the Qur'ān makes the treatment of orphans a testing ground for the veracity of a believer's faith: 'Do you see who it is who denies the religion? It is he who repulses the orphan.' (al-Mā^cūn, 107:1-2)

أرأيت الذي يكذب بالدين فذلك الذى يدع اليتيم.

The Prophet ﷺ is reported to have said: 'One who affectionately strokes the head of the orphan, God will reward him for every single hair he has touched.'[15]

من مسح على رأس اليتيم لم يمسحه إلا لله كان له في كل شعرة مرت عليها يده حسنات.

The Prophet ﷺ also stated, according to another *ḥadīth*, the following: 'By the one who sent me with the truth, God will not inflict torture on the Day of Judgment upon one who has been compassionate to the orphan.'[16]

والذى بعثنى بالحق لا يعذب الله يوم القيامة من رحم اليتيم.

NOTES

1. Al-Ghazālī, *Ḥuqūq al-Insān*, p. 54.
2. Al-Zuḥaylī has quoted five *ḥadīth* on the subject. See for details, al-Zuḥaylī, *al-Fiqh al-Islāmī*, VI, 421ff.
3. Shams al-Dīn Muḥammad al-Sarakhsī, *al-Mabsūṭ*, 15 vols., Beirut, Dār al-Maᶜrifah, 1406/1986, X, 210; Ismāᶜīl al-Badawī, *Daᶜā'im al-Ḥukm fi'l-Sharīᶜah al-Islāmiyyah wa'l-Nuẓūm al-Dustūriyyah al-Muᶜāṣirah*, Cairo, Dār al-Fikr al-ᶜArabī, 1400/1980, p. 524.
4. Muḥammad ibn Idrīs al-Shāfiᶜī, *Kitāb al-Umm*, ed. Muḥammad Sayyid Kaylāni, 2nd edn, 6 vols., Cairo, Musṭafā al-Bābī al-Ḥalabī, 1403/1983, VI, 266; Abū Zahrah, *Tanẓīm*, p. 135.
5. al-ᶜĪlī, *Ḥurriyyāt* , Cairo, Dār al-Fikr, n.d., p. 363.
6. Abū Zahrah, *Tanẓīm*, p. 107; al-ᶜĪlī, *Ḥurriyyāt*, p. 362.
7. ᶜAbd al-Qādir ᶜAwdah, *al-Tashrīᶜ al Jinā'ī al-Islāmī*, Beirut, Mu'assasat al-Risālah, 1403/1983, I, 446.
8. Al-Tabrīzī, ᶜAbd Allāh al-Khaṭīb, *Mishkāt al-Maṣabīḥ*, Eng. trans. James Robson, Lahore, Ashraf Press, n.d., vol. II, *ḥadīth* 3453.
9. Cf. al-Zuḥaylī, *Ḥuqūq al-Insān*, p. 144: Sibāᶜī, *al-Takāful al-Ijtimāᶜī*, p. 62.
10. See for details Ibn ᶜAbidin, *Ḥāshiyah*, vol. I, p. 119; Maḥmūd Shaltūt, *al-Islām: ᶜAqīdah wa Sharīᶜah*, Kuwait, Maṭbaᶜ Dār al-Qalam, 1966, pp. 209-212; al-Sibāᶜī, *al-Takāful al-Ijtimāᶜī*, pp. 60-70.

11. Abū Ḥāmid Muḥammad al-Ghazālī, *Iḥyā' ᶜUlūm al-Dīn*, 2nd edn, 5 vols., Cairo, Dār al-Fikr, 1400/1980, vol. II, p. 47; Shaltūt, *al-Islām: ᶜAqīdah wa Sharīᶜah*, pp. 203-204.

12. Al-Tabrizī, *Mishkāt* (Robson's trans.), vol. II, p. 1035. The Arabic text of the *ḥadīth* is not given.

13. Al-Nawawī, *Riyāḍ al-Ṣāliḥīn*, *ḥadīth* no. 359.

14. Muḥammad ibn Ismāᶜīl al-Bukhārī, *Ṣaḥīḥ al-Bukhārī*, Eng. trans. Muḥsin Khān, 6th edn, 9 vols., Lahore, Kazi Publication, 1986, VIII, 23, *ḥadīth* no. 34.

15. Zakī al-Dīn al-Mundhirī, *al-Targhīb wa'l-Tarhīb*, 2 vols., Cairo, Muṣṭafā al-Bābī al-Aalabī, 1373/1979, IV, 218.

16. Ibid., II, 161.

CHAPTER SIX

Dignity and Just Character (*ᶜAdālah*)

The upright character (*ᶜadālah*) of an individual is a proof of his distinction and dignity in the eyes of the law. In almost all spheres of public life, whether a person acts as a witness in a court, or as a trustee and guardian (*walī*) of the person or property of another, or is a qualified scholar and *mujtahid*, a trustee (*mutawallī*) of charitable endowments (*awqāf*), a government employee or a judge or head of state in each case a person must pass the test of *ᶜadālah*. The juristic manuals of *fiqh* specify the detailed criteria by which the *ᶜadālah* of a person is determined and established. What this means is that Islamic law generally envisages the Muslim community as a body whose affairs are administered by upright individuals. These are the bearers of the trust of *khilāfah* and the gatekeepers of justice, which are duties that only honourable individuals are qualified to undertake. It comes as no surprise therefore that the Qur'ān takes a serious view of any attack on the honour and good name of an upright individual.[1]

This is the theme, in fact, of a number of passages in the Qur'ān where insult, defamation, the calling of names, backbiting and derision are condemned, proscribed and penalised. The manner in which the Qur'ān speaks of these has led many a jurist to the conclusion that backbiting, for example, is a major sin, that is, one of the *kabā'ir*. For the Qur'ān speaks of backbiting in such terms as: 'Would any one of you wish to eat the flesh of his brother? Surely you would abhor it.' (al-Ḥujurāt, 49:12).

أيحب أحدكم أن يأكل لحم أخيه ميتا فكرهتموه.

Dignity is also violated by ridicule, defamation and sarcasm, which are proscribed in the Qur'ān:

> O you who believe! Let not some men among you laugh at others. It may be that the latter are better than the former. Nor let some women laugh at others. It may be that the latter are better than the former. Nor defame nor be sarcastic to each other, nor call each other by offensive nicknames. (al-Ḥujurāt, 49:11)

يا أيها الذين أمنوا لا يسخر قوم من قوم عسى أن يكونوا خيرا منهم ولا نساء من نساء عسى أن يكن خيرا منهن ولا تلمزوا أنفسكم ولا تنابزوا بالألقاب.

Slanderous accusation (*qadhf*) is one of the prescribed (*ḥudūd*) offences which the Qur'ān penalises with a mandatory punishment of eighty whip lashes (al-Nūr, 24:4). Even when the slanderous accuser (*qādhif*) is duly tried and punished, he is never again to be admitted as a witness in a court of justice. For the offence he committed may have inflicted irreparable damage to the good name and honour of his victim. According to another Qur'ānic proclamation, everyone is required to respect the dignity and good name of others. The text thus declares that 'those who love that scandal should circulate concerning those who believe, for them is a grievous chastisement in this world and the Hereafter' (al-Nūr, 24:19).

إنّ الذين يحبون أن تشيع الفاحشة في الذين آمنوا لهم عذاب أليم في الدنيا والآخرة.

The Qur'ān also forbids insulting disbelievers and 'those who call on other than God, lest they, exceeding the limits, revile God through ignorance' (al-Anᶜām, 6:108).

ولا تسبوا الذين يدعون من دون اللّه فيسبوا اللّه عدوا بغير علم.

Concealing the weaknesses of others and turning a blind eye to their failings is a consistent theme of the teachings of the Prophet ﷺ. Thus according to a *ḥadīth*, 'Anyone who conceals the weakness of another in this world, God will conceal their weakness in the Hereafter.'[2]

لايستر عبدا في الدنيا إلا ستره اللّه يوم القيامة.

The Prophet ﷺ declared on another occasion that 'humiliating a fellow Muslim is enough to make a Muslim an evil-doer'.[3]

بحسب أمرئ من شر أن يحقر أخاه المسلم.

According to another *ḥadīth* reported by Bukhārī and Muslim, the Prophet ﷺ said: 'One of the major sins that a man can commit is to insult his parents.' This statement provoked a question from the Companions, who asked: 'O Messenger of God! Does a man ever insult his parents?' The Prophet ﷺ replied '[Yes] when he insults another man's father or mother and this is reciprocated in return.'[4]

من أكبر الكبائر أن يسب الرجل والديه، قيل كيف يا رسول اللّه،
قال يسب الرجل أبا الرجل فيسب أباه، ويسب أمه.

It is stated in another *ḥadīth* that 'insulting a Muslim is inequity and fighting him is disbelief'.[5]

سباب المسلم فسوق وقتاله كفر.

The usage of the word '*kufr*' here is figurative, and indicates emphasis. The prohibition of insulting a Muslim applies equally to the followers of other faiths and to those who do not adhere to any religion.[6]

Respect for the dignity of others is a feature of the fraternity of the believers and solidarity within the rank of the *ummah*, which is more than mere conformity to form. It is an attitude of the Muslim personality and culture that must be observed not only in the external manifestation of conduct but in the thinking and attitudes of believers. The Prophet thus merely reiterated the words of the Qur'ān (al-Hujurāt, 49:12) when he warned the believers to 'beware of suspicion, for suspicion in some cases partakes of sin and may amount to the worst form of lying'.[7]

إياكم والظن فإن الظن أكذب الحديث.

The substance of this teaching is endorsed in another *ḥadīth* as follows: 'When you hear something that your brother might have said, give it the best interpretation until you find no other way of doing so.'

اذا بلغك عن أخيك شئ فاحمله على أحسنه حتى لا تجد له محملاً.

Imām Aḥmad ibn Ḥanbal commented on the correct meaning of this *ḥadīth*, saying that one should 'find an excuse for him by saying that maybe he said, or maybe he meant, such and such'.[8] Furthermore, on the same subject, the Prophet ﷺ declared in another *ḥadīth*:

> When a Muslim protects the honour of another at a time when the latter is attacked, God will protect him at a time when he desires protection. And when a man dishonours a Muslim where the latter is vulnerable to attack, God will dishonour the former at a time when he wants God's help.[9]

ما من أمرئ مسلم ينصر مسلما في موضع ينتهك فيه من عرضه وتستحل حرمته إلا نصره الله عزوجل في موطن يحب فيه نصره وما من أمرئ خذل مسلما في موطن تنتهك فيه حرمته إلا خذله الله في موضع يحب فيه نصرته.

In yet another *ḥadīth*, it is stated: 'Whoever protects the honour of his brother, God will protect his countenance against the blaze of fire on the Day of Judgment.'[10]

من رد عن عرض أخيه رد الله عن وجهه النار يوم القيامة.

The Prophet ﷺ has encouraged tolerance and latitude in the treatment of others in daily encounters, in trading and at all levels of interaction. Thus the Prophet ﷺ said in a *ḥadīth* : 'May the mercy of God be on one who is lenient when he sells, lenient when he buys, and lenient when he makes a demand.'[11]

رحم الله عبدا سمحا اذا باع، سمحا إذا إشترى، سمحا إذا اقتضى.

One who wishes the integrity of his faith to remain unblemished in the eyes of God, should avoid telling a white lie even in jest, and avoid acrimony and pointless squabbling that threatens to undermine the dignified treatment of others, even if the speaker is telling the truth. This is the purport of the following *ḥadīth* :

> Perfection in faith cannot be accomplished unless the believer abandons lying in the jokes he makes, and abandons acrimony even if he is truthful.[12]

لا يؤمن العبد الإيمان كله حتى يترك الكذب في المزاح ويترك المراء ولو كان صادقاً.

Indulgence in acrimonious bickering (*al-mirā'*, also known as *mumārāt*) has been denounced in a number of *ḥadīth*, as *mirā'* originates in scant regard for the dignity of others and undermines the social harmony that is a necessary ingredient of fraternity. The following *ḥadīth* promises distinction and spiritual reward for those who avoid *mirā'*:

> One who abandons *mirā'* even if he knows that he is right, a dwelling will be built for him in the highest echelons of Paradise, and one who avoids it while knowing that he is in the wrong, a dwelling will still be built for him in Paradise.[13]

من ترك المراء وهو محق بنى له البيت في أعلى الجنة ومن ترك المراء وهو مبطل بنى له البيت في ربض الجنة.

In yet another *ḥadīth* on the same subject, the Prophet ﷺ addressed the believers in the following terms: 'Avoid engaging in bitter exchanges with your brother, and do not ridicule him, or make him a promise that you do not honour.'[14]

ولا تمار أخاك ولا تمازحه ولا تعده موعدا فتخلفه.

NOTES

1. Cf. Mohammad H. Kamali, *Freedom of Expression in Islam*, 2nd edn, Cambridge, The Islamic Texts Society, 1997, pp. 12ff.

2. Al-Nawawī, *Riyāḍ al-Ṣāliḥīn*, *ḥadīth* no. 245.

3. Muslim ibn Ḥajj ibn Ḥajjāj al-Nishāpūrī, *Mukhtaṣar Ṣaḥīḥ Muslim*, ed. Muḥammad Nāṣir al-Dīn al-Albānī, 2 vols., Beirut, Dār al-Maktab al-Islāmī, 2nd edn, 1404/1984, p. 437, *ḥadīth* no. 1775.

4. Al-Tabrīizī, *Mishkāt*, vol. III, *ḥadīth* no. 4916.

5. Ibid., *ḥadīth* no. 4814.

6. See for details Kamali, *Freedom of Expression*, pp. 177ff.

7. Muslim, *Mukhtaṣar Ṣaḥīḥ Muslim*, p. 477, *ḥadīth* no. 1803.

8. Shams al-Dīn al-Maqdisī, *al-Ādāb al-Sharᶜiyyah wa'l-Minaḥ al-Marᶜiyyah,* Cairo, Maṭbaᶜat al-Manār, 1348AH, I, 340.

9. Al-Ghazālī, *Iḥyā' ᶜUlūm al-Dīn*, VI, 26; Idem, *Kitāb Ādāb al-Ulfa wa'l-Ukhuwwa wa'l-Ṣuḥba*, p. 369.

10. Al-Nawawī, *Riyāḍ al-Ṣāliḥīn*, p. 488, *ḥadīth* no. 153.

11. Aḥmad ibn ᶜAlī ibn Ḥajar al-ᶜAsqalānī, *Jawāhir Ṣaḥīḥ al-Bukhāri*, ed. ᶜIzz al-Dīn al-Sirwān, Beirut, Dār Iḥyā' al-ᶜUlūm, 1407/1987, *ḥadīth* no. 275.

12. Al-Maqdisī, *al-Ādāb al-Sharᶜiyyah*, I, 21.

13. Abū ᶜĪsā Muḥammad al-Tirmidhī, *Sunan al-Tirmidhī*, 3 vols., Beirut, Dār al-Fikr, 1400/1980, *ḥadīth* no. 1993; al-Ghazālī, *Iḥyā' ᶜUlūm al-Dīn*, V, 179.

14. Al-Tabrīizī, *Mishkāt*, vol. III, *ḥadīth* no. 4892.

CHAPTER SEVEN

Man and the Universe

Another manifestation of the dignified status of man in the eyes of the Creator is the subjugation of the entire created universe to his benefit and service. This is confirmed in the Qur'ān where God Most High declares in an open address to mankind: 'And He has subjected to [your use] all that is in the heavens and the earth [...]. Behold, in this there are signs for those who reflect.' (al-Jāthiyah, 45:13)

وسخرلكم ما في السماوات وما في الأرض جميعاً منه إنّ في ذلك لآيات لقوم يتفكرون.

References to the benefit and beauty of so many of God's creations also abound in the Qur'ān, for instance to the natural world, water, wind, plants and animals, the sun and the moon, all of which are made manageable for man's benefit and service, and added to this is the reminder that 'you are unable to count the favours that God has bestowed upon you' (Ibrāhīm, 14:34).

وإن تعدوا نعمة اللّه لا تحصوها.

And then we read the confirmation that 'He it is who made the earth manageable for you, so travel through its tracts and enjoy the sustenance He furnishes' (al-Mulk, 67:15).

هو الذى جعل لكم الأرض ذلولا فامشوا في مناكبها وكلوا من رزقه.

This *āyah* clearly encourages human initiative and effort to utilise the resources of the earth through all legitimate means. One might add here perhaps that the phrase 'enjoy the sustenance' implies that the utilisation of the earth and its resources should be for human need and welfare, and not, as it were, for questionable and ultimately destructive purposes. In their capacity as God's vicegerent on the earth, human beings are the trustees and custodians of the earth and are therefore responsible for the balanced and careful management of its resources. This is the clear message of another *āyah* wherein God Most High entrusts man with the authority to manage and utilise the resource of the earth:

> It is We who have placed you with authority on earth, and provided you with means for the fulfilment of your life. (al-Aʿrāf, 7:10)

ولقد مكناكم في الأرض وجعلنا لكم فيها معايش.

To add emphasis to this, the text then poses the question:

> Do you not see that God has subjected to your [use] all that is in the heavens and the earth and has made His bounties flow to you in exceeding measure [both] seen and unseen? (Luqmān, 31:20)

أولم تروا أن اللّه سخرلكم مافي السماوات وما في الأرض وأسبغ
عليكم نعمه ظاهرة وباطنة.

In things that the human senses can apprehend, and even when the senses fall short of apprehending, God's favours are to be seen everywhere. God has granted man the faculty to subdue the forces of nature with knowledge and reason, all of which provides evidence that man's status and destiny are noble to the highest degree.

Subjugation (*taskhīr*) of the universe to the benefit and service of mankind is one of the major themes of the Qur'ān, which contains both general and specific references to the various aspects of subjugation. Thus it is declared that 'God subjugated to you the rivers, and He subjugated to you the sun and the moon, constant in their courses, and subjugated to you the night and days' (Ibrāhīm, 14:32-33)

وسخّر لكم الانهار وسخّر لكم الشّمس والقمر دآئبين وسخّر لكم الّيل والنّهار

and 'He subjugated to you all that is in the heavens' (al-Jāthiyah, 45:13).

وسخّر لكم ما في السّماوات

The Arabic word *taskhīr* implies the ability to derive benefit and service without any remuneration or return, such as in the case of an animal one owns. Two basic conclusions have been drawn from the Qur'ānic references to *taskhīr*, one of which is that nothing in the world of creation is beyond the reach and capacity of man. Subjugation in this sense implies that permissibility is the basic norm of *Sharīʿah*, which means it is permissible for mankind to utilise and harness all the resources of the universe. The second conclusion drawn here is that all people are equally entitled to benefit from the resources of the universe. This is evident from the general language of the text, which consistently addresses the whole of mankind without any exception. No nation, group of nations, or section or class of *Homo sapiens* has therefore a superior claim to the resources of the universe beyond their geographical borders. It follows that protection of the environment, fighting pollution and natural calamities is a shared responsibility for mankind. Since human beings are shared beneficiaries of the natural resources of the earth and the world beyond, they are also jointly responsible for the adversities that are encountered.

The evidence that is reviewed here also lends support to another conclusion: since everything in the created world is subjected to man's benefit, then for man to bend so low as to worship (as some men do) stones, trees and animals, is tantamount to a denial of his inherent dignity.

CHAPTER EIGHT

Dignity and Freedom

The dignity of man is manifested, perhaps more than anything else, in his freedom of conscience, moral autonomy and judgement.[1] The Qur'ān overrules compulsion, which violates dignity, even in the acceptance or rejection of Islam itself: 'There shall be no compulsion in religion' (al-Baqarah, 2:256)

لا إكراه في الدين.

is the clarion call and motto of the Qur'ān. Invitation to the faith and *da'wah* must comply with the spirit of sincere advice and dignified persuasion. The Qur'ān has in many places addressed the Prophet ﷺ by reiterating that his task is confined to warning, the giving of advice and guidance, and that he has no authority to encroach on people's freedom of choice. Thus it is declared in the Qur'ān that, 'The truth has come from your Lord: let him who will, believe, and let him who will, reject it' (al-Kahf, 18:29)

وقل الحق من ربكم فمن شاء فليؤمن ومن شاء فليكفر.

and 'Anyone who accepts guidance does so for his own good, and if he wants to go astray, then tell him that "I am only a warner"' (al-Naml, 27:92).

فمن اهتدى فإنما يهتدى لنفسه ومن ضل فقل إنما أنا من المنذرين.

The same message is repeated in several other places, where appeals are made to the rational choice and judgement of man. The Qur'ān thus typically delivers a message and then reminds its reader that this message is meant for those who think and investigate and those who exercise their reason and considered judgement (*yatafakkarūn, yatadabbarūn, yanẓurūn, yatazakkarūn, yaᶜqilūn*) and so forth. Religious guidance is, in other words, given, propagated and expounded, but it may not be enforced by anything other than sound and sincere advice.[2]

The *Sharīᶜah* entitles the individual to say what he or she pleases, provided that the words uttered do not amount to blasphemy, insult, slander, or incitement to sin. In the affirmative sense, the *Sharīᶜah* encourages freedom of expression in a variety of ways, including the promotion of good and prevention of evil (*ḥisbah*), sincere advice (*naṣīḥah*), consultation (*shūrā*), personal reasoning (*ijtihād*) and the freedom to criticise government leaders (*ḥurriyyat al-muᶜāraḍah*).[3]

The Qur'ānic principle of *ḥisbah* provides a basic framework for the moral autonomy of the individual. When someone witnesses an evil being committed, he or she is entitled to take a moral stance, and then to intervene, prevent and denounce it as far as possible through action, and failing that, through speech, and finally, as a last resort, through inward denunciation. This is the subject of a *ḥadīth* which states:

> If any of you sees something evil, he should set it right by his hand; if he is unable to do so, then by his tongue; if he is unable to do even that, then let him denounce it in his heart. But this is the weakest form of faith.[4]

من رأى منكم منكرا فليغيره بيده فإن لم يستطع فبلسانه فإن لم يستطع فبقلبه وذلك أضعف الإيمان.

A correct implementation of *ḥisbah* takes for granted the freedom of the individual to formulate and express an opinion on an issue. Muslim jurists have addressed in detail the manner and method by which *ḥisbah* should be implemented and enforced. The most important of the several requirements of *ḥisbah* is that the person who carries it out must do so from a position of knowledge; he or she must act on the basis of a definite probability that the attempt will succeed and will not cause an evil greater than the one being prevented; and also that this prescription is carried out with courtesy and restraint. *Ḥisbah* normally begins with a declaration of the nature of the conduct in question (*taʿrif*) in words that draw attention, then it proceeds to kind admonition (*al-waʿẓ*), and then to words that are expressive of denunciation, such as 'O tyrant', 'O ignorant', 'Don't you fear God'; and the last stage of *ḥisbah* consists of expressing anger or the use of force when absolutely necessary.[5] The Qur'ānic principle of *naṣīḥah*, too, encourages the individual to give sincere advice to others, including government leaders, if he or she is convinced of the essential benefit of this advice. The centrality of this principle to Islam is highlighted in a *ḥadīth* wherein the Prophet ﷺ announces simply that 'religion is good advice–*al-dīnu al-naṣīḥatu*',[6] which means that *naṣīḥah* is a pillar of religion. The moral autonomy of the individual finds further support in a *ḥadīth* in which the Prophet instructs the believers to 'tell the truth even if it be unpleasant',

قل الحق ولو كان مرا.

and declares in another *ḥadith* that 'the best form of *jihād* is to tell a word of truth to an oppressive ruler'.[7]

أفضل الجهاد كلمة حق عند سلطان جائر.

According to yet another *ḥadīth*, 'there is no obedience in sin, obedience is found in righteous conduct'.[8]

لا طاعة في معصية إنّما الطاعة في المعروف.

These and many other aspects of the teachings of the Qur'ān and *Sunnah* confirm man's liberty of conscience as an inherent aspect of his dignity, and dignity as the basic right of every individual. The liberty of the human conscience as envisaged by Islam is clearly expressed elsewhere in a *ḥadīth* in which the Prophet ﷺ is reported to have said: 'When you see my community afraid of addressing a tyrant with "O tyrant", then it is not worth belonging to it anymore.'[9]

إذا رأيت أمتي تهاب أن تقول للظالم يا ظالم فقد تؤدع منها.

The *Sunnah* of the Prophet ﷺ also enjoins the believers to avoid the humiliation that arises from unwarranted silence. They should, instead, stand for a good cause and speak for it when the occasion presents itself. Thus the Prophet declared in a *ḥadīth* :

> 'Let no one humiliate themselves'. Upon hearing this the Companions asked: 'How does one do that, O Messenger of God?' Then the Prophet said: 'When someone sees an occasion in which he should speak out for the sake of God but he does not, then God Most High will tell him on the Day of Judgment: what stopped you from speaking on that issue? And when the person answers: the fear of people, then God says: you should have feared Me and put Me above fearing others.'[10]

لا يحقر أحدكم نفسه قالوا يا رسول اللّه كيف يحقر أحدنا نفسه؟ قال يرى أمرا للّه عليه مقال ثم لا يقول فيه، فيقول اللّه عز وجل يوم القيامة: ما منعك أن تقول في كذاكذا، فيقول خشية الناس، فيقول: فإياى كنت أحق أن تخشى.

The moral autonomy of the individual is a necessary consequence of his freedom and responsibility in Islam. This is clearly conveyed in a *ḥadīth* which proclaims: 'Every one of you is a guardian and is responsible for what is in his custody. The Imām is a guardian and responsible for his subjects; a man is the guardian of his family and responsible for its members; a woman is the guardian of her husband's home and children and she is responsible for them.'[11]

ألا كلكم راع وكلكم مسئول عن رعيته، فالإمام على الناس راع وهو مسئول عن رعيته و الرجل راع على أهل بيته وهو مسئول عن رعيته والمرأة راعية على أهل بيت زوجها و ولده وهى مسئولة عنهم.

Commentators have often identified Islam as essentially communitarian in ethos, in the sense that it gives priority to the common good of the community in the event of a conflict of interests between the individual and the community. This is true to a large extent, but not so far as to suggest that the individual is totally subsumed by social purpose and interest. Islam is first and foremost a religion and a moral code which, like all religions, must take the individual as its primary nexus. Virtually all of Islam's basic teachings are addressed to the individual. This is borne out by the familiar Qur'ānic address to the believers (*yā ayyuhalladhīna āmanū*), which takes the individual believer as the main audience for its messages. It is through reforming the individual that Islam seeks to achieve its social goals. Whether one speaks of *ḥisbah* or of *naṣīḥah* or of trust (*amānah*), of freedom, responsibility (*taklīf*), the lawful and the forbidden (*ḥalāl, ḥarām*), or of the goals and purposes, that is, the *maqāṣid* of *Sharīʿah*, the focus of all of these is the individual. There is often, however, a convergence of values between the individual and the community, and discussing the one in isolation from the other is neither accurate nor sound. It remains to be said nevertheless that the idea of common good, or *maṣlaḥah*, is inherently relative (*nisbī, iḍāfī*), and often involves a compromise of some sort between individual and social interests, even in cases of potential conflict between them. The *Sharīʿah* would normally not sacrifice the basic rights and liberties of the individual and his human dignity and honour in the name of common good, or of communal interest and *maṣlaḥah*. The individual is thus seen, not just as a member of the community and subservient to its will, but as a morally autonomous agent who plays a distinctive role in shaping the community's sense of direction and purpose. This can also be seen in the conditions that the Qur'ān and *Sunnah* have attached to the individual's duty of obedience to the government, and the right he is simultaneously granted to dispute the rulers regarding community affairs (cf. al-Nisā', 4:59). The individual is thus required to obey the ruler, on condition, however, that the ruler obeys the *Sharīʿah*. The individual is also entitled, by the explicit terms of a number of *ḥadīth*, to disobey a command that is a blatant violation of the law and falls foul of the basic values and objectives of Islam.

Another manifestation of the freedom of conscience in relation to personal dignity, enshrined in the *Sharīʿah*, that may briefly be mentioned here is that Islam does not seek to apply its own laws to the followers of other faiths. Islam recognises the validity of other great religions and permits their followers who reside in Muslim territories to practice their own laws, especially in matters of personal status, custom and culture. Some of the prohibitions of *Sharīʿah*, such as those pertaining to the consumption of alcohol and pork, do not apply to the followers of other faiths. Muslim jurists have also expressed reservations in regard to the application of the prescribed penalties (*ḥudūd*) and expiations (*kaffārāt*) to non-Muslims. For these laws involve a devotional (*taᶜabbudī*) aspect with which non-Muslims are not expected to comply. Since faith is primarily a matter of conviction, then to impose punitive ordinances on a person contrary to his conviction is bound to violate his personal dignity, and the *Sharīᶜah* does not impose or allow this.

NOTES

1. Cf. Muḥammad al-Bahī, *al-Dīn wa'l-Dawlah min Tawjīhāt al-Qur'ān al-Karīm*, Beirut, Dār al-Fikr, 1391/1971, p. 565; Yusrī, *Ḥuqūq al-Insān*, p. 27.
2. Cf. Muḥammad ᶜAmmārah, *al-Islām wa Ḥuqūq al-Insān: Ḍarūrāt lā Ḥuqūq*, Cairo, Dār al-Shurūq, 1409/1989, pp. 27-28
3. There is a section on each of these in Kamali, *Freedom of Expression*, pp. 28-61.
4. Muslim, *Mukhtaṣar Ṣaḥīḥ Muslim*, *ḥadīth* no. 34.
5. Al-Ghazālī, *Iḥyā' ᶜUlūm al-Dīn*, II, 329ff.
6. Muslim, *Mukhtaṣar Ṣaḥīḥ Muslim*, *Kitāb al-Imān al-Dīn al-Naṣīḥa.*
7. Muḥammad ibn Yazīd al-Qazwīnī ibn Mājah, *Sunan Ibn Mājah*, 5 vols., Istanbul, Cagri Yayinlari, 1401/1981, *Kitāb al-Fitan, b. maᶜrūf wa nahy ᶜan al-munkar.*
8. Al-Tabrīzī, *Mishkāt*, vol. II, *ḥadīth* no. 3665.
9. Jalāl al-Dīn al-Suyūṭī, *al-Jāmiᶜ al-Ṣaghīr*, 4th edn, 2 vols., Cairo, Muṣṭafā al-Bābī al-Ḥalabī, 1954, I, 41; Aḥmad ibn Ḥanbal, *Fihris Aḥādīth Musnad al-Imām Ibn Ḥanbal*, compiled by Abū Hājr Zaghlūl, Beirut, Dār al-Kutub, 1386/1966, II, 163.
10. Ibn Mājah, *Sunan, Kitāb al-Fitan, b. maᶜrūf wa nahy ᶜan al-munkar.*
11. Al-Bukhārī, *Ṣaḥīḥ al-Bukhārī*, vol. IX, *ḥadīth* no. 252.

CHAPTER NINE

Commitment to Equality

Another manifestation of the dignity of man in Islam is its insistence on the essential equality of every member of the human race. All are equal in the eyes of God regardless of race, colour and religion. No man has a claim to superiority over another, and there is no recognition in Islam of a class or caste system, a superior race, a chosen people or any related concept. Man's inherent dignity is sacrosanct and the only ground of superiority recognised in the Qur'ān is God-consciousness (*taqwā*), as the following *āyah* declares:

> O mankind, We have created you from a male and a female and made you into tribes and nations so that you may know one another. The most noble of you before God is the most God-conscious of you. (al-Ḥujurāt, 49:13)

يا أيها الناس إنا خلقناكم من ذكر و أنثى و جعلناكم شعوبا و قبائل
لتعارفوا إنّ أكرمكم عند اللّه أتقاكم.

The essential equality of humanity necessitates equality in human rights, including the right to justice, the equal protection of the law, equality in respect of education and employment, and the enjoyment of basic liberties.[1] Equality before the law and before the courts of justice was the central theme of the directive of the second Caliph, ʿUmar ibn al-Khaṭṭāb, who wrote in his renowned letter to his judges to 'treat the people [*al-nās*] equally in your courtroom, in your presence and in your judgement so that the strong do not become covetous of your favour, nor do the weak despair of your justice'.[2]

The Prophet ﷺ himself manifested the egalitarian spirit of Islam in his dealings with the people around him. The Qur'ān has in several places directed the Prophet ﷺ to declare to his followers that 'I am but a human being like the rest of you' (Fuṣṣilāt, 41:6).

إنما أنا بشر مثلكم.

The Prophet ﷺ and the Rightly-Guided Caliphs left behind a legacy that was distinctly egalitarian. The Prophet ﷺ did not claim any personal privileges for himself and preferred to be treated as one among equals. When he sat with his Companions, he sat in such a way that he would not be recognised. Then the Companions requested the Prophet ﷺ to make himself prominent so as to be recognised, which is why they built for him a pulpit. Al-Ghazālī has quoted the *ḥadīth*, reported by Abū Dāwūd, in which the Prophet ﷺ warned of the punishment in the Hereafter for 'those who love to be glorified by other men'.[3]

Furthermore, the Prophet ﷺ did not allow people to stand up in his honour, and directed his followers against it. Thus the Prophet ﷺ said in a *ḥadīth*: 'A man should not make another man stand up for him in order to take his seat.'[4]

لا يقيم الرجل الرجل من مجلسه ثم يجلس فيه.

A second *ḥadīth* on the same subject recapitulates this point and then adds: 'But one should make room and spread out'

ولكن تفسحوا وتوسعوا.

so as to make space for one who enters a meeting.[5] Similarly, the Prophet ﷺ did not allow his people to address him by grand honorific titles and refused to be treated with the pomp and ceremony that was in vogue at the Persian and Bizantine courts of the time. He is on record to have stated, for example, 'I am neither a King nor a tyrant' and advised his Companions not to glorify anyone but God Most High. The head of state, in Muslim constitutional theory, is consequently granted no special privileges and is held accountable for his conduct in the same way as an ordinary citizen.[6]

Another feature of the teachings of Islam is that believers are encouraged to treat each other with dignity when they interact. The Qur'ān thus enjoins the Muslims to 'speak to the people in good words' (al-Baqarah, 2:83)

وقولوا للناس حسنا.

and 'guide others to be pleasant in speech' (al-Hajj, 22:24).

وهدوا الى الطيب من القول.

Moreover, the recurrent Qur'ānic theme which encourages courteous speech (*qawlan maʿrūfan*) when addressing one's parents (al-Isrā', 17:23), the poor and the indigent (al-Nisā', 4:8) and the people at large (al-Isrā', 17:53 and *passim*) manifests Islam's outlook on human dignity. Furthermore, it is reported in a *ḥadīth* that a Muslim has a right over another Muslim in six matters, namely, 'to return his greeting (*salām*), to accept his invitation, to visit him in sickness, to give him sincere advice (*naṣīḥah*), to say "God have mercy on you" when he sneezes, and attend his funeral'.[7] The Prophet's Companions and the Rightly-Guided Caliphs after him reflected the same attitudes in their dealings with people and in the manner in which they behaved themselves. The early Caliphs thus shunned claiming for themselves what the Prophet ﷺ had neither practised nor advised. The Rightly-Guided Caliphs thus denied themselves court ceremonials and privileges of the kind that violate the personal dignity of the individual or which might belittle their image and confidence.

NOTES

1. Cf. Muḥammad Rajā' Mutajallī, *al-Ḥurriyyāt wa'l-Ḥuqūq fi'l-Islām*, Rābitat al-ʿAlam al-Islāmī bi-Makkah al-Mukarramah: Dār al-Ṣaḥāfah wa'l-Nashr, 1407/1987, p. 23.
2. Quoted in al-Sibāʿī, *Ishtirākiyyat al-Islām*, p. 69.
3. Al-Ghazālī, *Iḥyā' ʿUlūm al-Dīn*, II, 381.
4. Al-Bukhārī, *Ṣaḥīḥ al-Bukhārī*, vol. VIII, *ḥadīth* no. 286.
5. Ibid., *ḥadīth* no. 287.
6. Muḥammad ibn Jarīr al-Ṭabarī, *Ta'rīkh al-Rusul wa'l-Mulūk*, Cairo, al-Maṭbaʿah al-Tijāriyyah, 1358/1939, III, 584; Yusrī, *Ḥuqūq al-Insān*, p. 31.
7. Al-Tabrīzī, *Mishkāt*, vol. I, *ḥadīth* no. 1525.

CHAPTER TEN

Commitment to Virtue

The Qur'ānic principles of *ḥisbah* commit both the individual and the community to the promotion of good and the prevention of evil. There are several *āyāt* in the Qur'ān on this, but one that is frequently cited is as follows:

> You are the best community evolved for mankind, enjoining what is right and forbidding what is wrong and you believe in God. (Āl ʿImrān, 3:110)

> كنتم خير أمّة أخرجت للنّاس تأمرون بالمعروف وتنهون عن المنكر وتؤمنون باللّه

The dignified standing of the community in the eyes of God is thus conditional on faith in God and a firm commitment to *ḥisbah*. The community as a whole and its individual members incur blame when they fail to prevent an evil that they observe, and they merit praise when they do prevent it, or succeed in promoting a good cause. It is on this account that Abū Zahrah describes the Muslim community as *ummah fāḍilah* (virtuous community).[1] The quest for virtue here is a responsibility of the community, which is why *ḥisbah* is identified as a collective obligation (*farḍ kifā'ī*) of the community as a whole and not a personal obligation of every member thereof. The duty is fulfilled even if some individuals attempt it, but all will incur a sin if it is ignored entirely.

The Prophet ﷺ instructed the believers in a *ḥadīth* that: 'You must not underestimate the value of *maʿrūf* even if it be by facing your brother with a smile, or by giving water to the thirsty.'[2]

لا تحقّرنّ من المعروف شيئا ولو أن تلقى اخاك ووجهك اليه منبسط، ولو أن تفرغ من دلوك في اناء المستسقي.

To be good to others, treat them fairly, and have a pleasant word for them all partake of *maʿrūf* and merit spiritual reward. The Prophet ﷺ has stressed this when he said: 'Good morals are the heaviest of all things that are weighed [on the Day of Judgement].'[3]

إنّ اثقل ما يوضع في الميزان الخلق الحسن.

The Qur'ān epitomises the essence of *maʿrūf* when it proclaims:

> Good deeds and evil ones can never be equal. Repel evil with good, then you will see that even one with whom you had enmity will become as though he were an intimate friend. (Fuṣṣilāt, 41:34)

لا تستوى الحسنة ولا السيّئة، ادفع بالّتي هي أحسن، فإذا الّذي بينك وبينه عداوة كأنّه وليّ حميم.

This is evidently not a directive but moral advice addressed to those who seek to excel in virtue. The normal course that is elsewhere expounded in the Qur'ān allows for reciprocal treatment of like for like, which is the essence of justice, as in the following *āyah*:

> The recompense of evil is an evil like it, but one who forgives and makes amends, His reward will be with God, and He does love not the unjust (al-Shūra, 42:40).

وجزاء سيّئة سيّئة مثلها، فمن عفا واصلح فأجره على اللّه إنّه لا يحب الظّالمين.

Reciprocity is the normal course of law and justice, but moral excellence is achieved not necessarily through reciprocity, but through forgiveness and averting hostility and conflict. To bring harmony where conflict is normally expected grasps the spirit of *maʿrūf* and ranks highly on the scale of virtue.

Ḥisbah may not, however, be used as a tool in the hands of the self-righteous, or as a pretext for harassing others and attempting to expose their failings, as the Qur'ān provides:

> The believers, men and women, are friends and protectors of one another, enjoining good and preventing evil; they maintain prayer and pay the *zakāh*. (al-Tawba, 9:71)

والمؤمنون والمؤمنات بعضهم أولياء بعض يأمرون بالمعروف
وينهون عن المنكر

Ḥisbah must therefore be conducted in the spirit of friendship and protection against abuse. *Ḥisbah* is a collective obligation, yet it does not warrant persistent interference in the private lives of individuals. One of the rules of *ḥisbah* thus has it that when evil is committed in private and the perpetrator neither declares it nor is he persistent, then it should not be revealed, and the best advice for others would be to turn a blind eye to it. This is the purport of a *ḥadīth* stating that: 'When a sin is concealed [from the public eye] it harms only its perpetrator, but when it is publicised and not condemned, it harms the community as a whole.'[4]

المعصية اذا خفيت لم تضر إلا صاحبها ولكن اذا ظهر فلم تنكرت
اضرت العامة.

The advice of tolerance that is conveyed in this *ḥadīth* is evidently not extended to the perpetrator of evil who broadcasts his evil deed, and by doing so compromises the community's vision of itself and its collective commitment to virtue. When the evildoer is left to his own devices and the community lowers its vigilance, its virtuous aspirations are likely to be compromised. When this happens, one can hardly expect anything other than the consequences of one's negligence, as the Qur'ān confirms:

> God will not change the condition of the people unless they actually change it themselves. (al-Raʿd, 13:11)

إنّ اللّه لا يغيّر ما بقوم حتى يغيّروا ما بأنفسهم.

'It is the right of the people in Islam and also their duty', wrote al-Qaraḍāwī, 'to give advice to their rulers to rectify them when they deviate, and to prevent them from committing evil.'[5] In a reference to previous nations who neglected this, the Qur'ān proclaims that 'they restrained not one another from the evil they did, and they fell into it all of them' (al-Mā'idah, 5:79).

كانوا لا يتناهون عن منكر فعلوه لبئس ما كانوا يفعلون.

A certain misunderstanding arose among the Companions over the purport of the following Qur'ānic text: 'O believers you have to take charge of your own selves. He who errs cannot injure you if you are rightly guided' (al-Mā'idah, 5:105).

ياايّها الّذين آمنوا عليكم انفسكم لا يضرّكم من ضلّ إذا اهتديتم.

The first Caliph Abū Bakr attempted to rectify a certain misreading of this text, which implied that people should take care of their own deeds. In one of his sermons, the Caliph addressed the people and said that they were reading this verse in a way that was not correct. For he had heard the Messenger of God ﷺ explain that 'when the people witness an evil and do not attempt to change it, they bring themselves close to the point where God includes them among those punished for that evil'. [6]

إنّ النّاس إذا رأووا المنكر فلم يغيّروه اوشك أن يعمّهم اللّه بعقاب منه.

The details of what is actually virtuous and what may be considered to be evil is often specified and indicated by the *Sharīʿah*, but not always. In the event where the *Sharīʿah* is silent on a matter that may fall into the twilight zone of partaking of a measure both of good and of some evil then prevention of evil takes priority over the pursuit of good. Promoting a virtuous image and ideal is sometimes given priority over the *Sharīʿah* rules of justice. To illustrate this, the rules of justice advise reciprocal treatment (*muʿāmalah bi'l-mithl*) especially in the sphere of international relations and regarding prisoners of war. But Muslim jurists have held that reciprocal treatment should be moderated and subjected to moral and humanitarian considerations. If in times of war the enemy forces resort to heinous acts of killing women and children, maiming their victims and destroying animals and trees, their conduct should not be reciprocated and neither unnecessary violence nor degradation should be inflicted in the name of reciprocity. This is because commitment to virtue is a basic postulate of human relations in Islam. It is thus held impermissible to exceed the limits of propriety and indulge in depraved and objectionable behaviour that violates human dignity.[7]

Two other aspects of the quest for virtue in Islam are manifested in humility (*al-ḥayā'*) and in leniency (*al-rifq*). Humility and meekness (*al-ḥayā'*) is one of the recognised virtues of Islam so much so that the Prophet ﷺ declared in a *ḥadīth* that '*ḥayā'* is goodness from beginning to end [*al-ḥayā' khayrun kullih*]'. The unqualified terms of this pronouncement indicate that no one should attempt to impose any restrictions on *ḥayā'*. The proverbial Arabic phrase 'When you have abandoned *ḥayā'*, then do what you wish [*idhā lam tastaḥi fa's-naᶜ mā shi'ta*]'[8] grasps the meaning of this *ḥadīth*. *Ḥayā'* as such is the opposite of selfishness, and is closely related to self-restraint. *Ḥayā'* is also a component of piety (*taqwā*) which is itself a major theme of the moral teachings of Islam. *Ḥayā'* is not self-effacement nor is it indicative of a lack of courage. The Prophet obviously gave *ḥayā'* a degree of prominence when he said in a *ḥadīth* that 'every religion has a certain ethos of its own and the ethos of Islam is *al-ḥayā'*'.[9]

لكل دين خلق و خلق الاسلام الحياء.

There is a difference between temerity (*al-jubn*) and humility (*al-ḥayā'*) in that the former conceals what ought to be declared whereas the latter conceals what ought to be concealed. To conceal that which would otherwise be abrasive and dishonourable partakes of *ḥayā'*. *Ḥayā'* is also a moral concept and it does not therefore imply condoning criminality or other prohibited things. Having said this, it will be noted that even with reference to criminal conduct, especially the prescribed *ḥudūd* offences, magnanimity and latitude is recommended prior to trial and arrest. Offences of a personal type, such as adultery and wine-drinking, that are not yet reported to the authorities may be concealed if this is deemed to be the right course of action to take. At this stage, it is advisable not to publicise the offence unless the perpetrator shows a lack of remorse and broadcasts it himself. The offender will then be regarded as the broadcaster of evil (*mujāhir bi'l-maᶜāṣī*) for whom forgiveness and concealment are not recommended. But these are the limits of magnanimity and tolerance. Once an offence has been reported, the law must take its course and the moral advice of tolerance and *ḥayā'* may not intervene in the process of law.

What has been said so far actually brings us close to yet another aspect of the moral ethos of Islam, which should be mentioned before concluding this discussion. I am referring here to leniency (*al-rifq*), which I have referred to before but mention it again as it takes a particularly high profile in the teachings of Islam. Leniency is recommended, like *al-ḥayā'*, in all human relations, even in the conduct of judges and law enforcement authorities. There is a clear and unequivocal acknowledgement that leniency can achieve virtue and beauty where severity can never achieve them, and this is why Islam recognises *al-rifq* as an integral part of its ethos. The two *ḥadīth* that I quote below are self explanatory on the value of *al-rifq*:

> Gentleness fails not to create beauty in everything, and it is not taken away from anything without causing ugliness.
>
> الرفق لا يكون في شيء الا زانه ولا ينزع من شيء الا شانه.
>
> God loves gentleness and gives through gentleness what He gives, not through harshness.[10]
>
> انّ اللّه يحبّ الرفق وهو يعطي في الرفق ما لم يعط في العنف.

Based on the clear teaching of yet another *ḥadīth*, the Muslim judge is advised not to be too eager in the infliction of penalties. The judge is thus instructed to 'drop the *ḥudūd* penalties in all cases of doubt' (*idra'u al-ḥudūda bi'l-shubhāt*). To make an error on the side of leniency is preferable to making it on the side of harshness. To punish an innocent person or a first offender, or one who may be remorseful of his failing, with severity and harshness is seen tantamount to the miscarriage of justice, and the judge is therefore strongly advised to consider leniency, or even granting a pardon, when this seems appropriate to him and in harmony with the virtuous ideals of Islam.

NOTES

1. Abū Zahrah, *al-Mujtama*ᶜ *al-Insānī*, p. 137.
2. Quoted by Tāqi al-Dīn ibn Taymiyyah, *al-Siyāsah al-Shar*ᶜ*iyyah fī Iṣlāḥ al-Rā*ᶜ*ī wa'l-Rā*ᶜ*iyyah*, 2nd edn, Cairo, Dār al-Kitāb al-ᶜArabī, 1951, p. 128.
3. Ibid.
4. Quoted in Ibn Taymiyyah, *al-Siyāsah al-Shar*ᶜ*iyyah*, p. 68.
5. Yūsuf al-Qaraḍāwī, *Min Fiqh al-Dawlah fi'l-Islām*, Cairo, Dār al-Shurūq, 1417/1997, p. 148.
6. Quoted in Ibn Taymiyyah, *al-Siyāsah al-Shar*ᶜ*iyyah*, p. 68.
7. Abū Zahrah, *al-Mujtama*ᶜ *al-Insānī*, p. 202.
8. Ibid., p. 139.
9. Ibid.
10. Both of these *ḥadīth* appear in Ibn Taymiyyah, *al-Siyāsah al-Shar*ᶜ*iyyah*, p. 145. See also Muslim, *Mukhtaṣar Ṣaḥīḥ Muslim*, p. 474, *ḥadīth* nos.1783 and 1784.

CHAPTER ELEVEN

Accountability in Government

The *locus* of political authority in Islam is the community of believers, the *ummah,* and its government is established in office through the people's pledge of allegiance (*bay*ᶜ*ah*) and consultation (*shūrā*). In political theory, the head of state is the people's representative (*wākil*) and trustee, who assumes office by means of the contract of agency (*wakālah*), and the government is under an obligation to consult the community in the conduct of its affairs. Leaders, caliphs and governors must prove their merit through stewardship and avoid the temptation of arrogating dignity and honour to themselves alone. Being the principal party (*muwakkil*) to the contract, the *ummah* is consequently entitled to depose a deviant leader who indulges in criminality and evil and no longer enjoys the trust and loyalty of the people. Furthermore, the collective will and consensus (*ijmā*ᶜ) of the community is the only recognised source, in the legal theory of *uṣūl al-fiqh,* of binding legislation next to the Qur'ān and authentic *Sunnah*. What could be more honourable than the affirmation, in Islam, that the will and consensus of the community stands next in authority to the will of God Most High and the normative *Sunnah* of the Prophet ﷺ?

General evidence in the Qur'ān and the *Sunnah*, and in the precedent of the Rightly-Guided Caliphs, is clearly supportive of the accountability of government. The Qur'ānic principle of *ḥisbah*—enjoining good and forbidding evil—(cf. Āl Imrān, 3:104 and 110; al-Tawbah, 9:71), to which reference has already been made, is a broad principle of public law that entitles everyone to take a vigilant attitude towards corruption and abuse. The *Sunnah* further elaborated on this, and has accordingly envisaged three stages in the implementation of *ḥisbah*, the first of which authorises the direct observer to take action against an evil being committed, provided that he is actually able to do so. If this is not possible, one may verbally denounce an evil, and finally, in cases where verbal denunciation is also unfeasible, one may silently denounce it inwardly and disassociate oneself from it. These three stages of *ḥisbah* are expounded in the following *ḥadīth*:

> If any of you sees something evil, he should set it right by his hand; if he is unable to do so, then by his tongue; and if he is unable to do even that, then [let him denounce it] in his heart. But this is the weakest form of faith.[1]

من رأى منكم منكرا فليغيّره بيده، فإن لم يستطع فبلسانه، فإن لم يستطع فبقلبه، وذلك اضعف الايمان.

The head of state and government officials are under an obligation, as the Qur'ān provides in another *āyah*, to discharge their trust faithfully and justly:

> God commands you to render the trusts to whom they belong, and when you judge among people, judge with justice. (al-Nisā', 4:58)

إن اللّه يأمركم أن تؤدّوا الأمانات إلى أهلها وإذا حكمتم بين النّاس أن تحكموا بالعدل.

Reports have it that this *āyah* was revealed concerning the appointment of government officials and the designation of trusts (*amānāt*) to government office. Contained herein, therefore, is the idea of accountability to God and to the community of believers. This is also confirmed in a *ḥadīth* which the Prophet ﷺ is reported to have pronounced in response to a request by the renowned Companion, Abū Dharr al-Ghaffārī. He is reported to have asked the Prophet ﷺ if he could be employed to a government post. To this the Prophet ﷺ replied: 'O Abū Dharr! This is a trust and you are weak; it brings remorse on the Day of Judgement unless it is rightly undertaken and duly discharged.'[2]

يا ابا ذر، انّك ضعيف وانّها امانة، وانّها يوم القيامة خزى و ندامة إلا من اخذها بحقها وادّى الّذي عليه فيها.

The Qur'ān makes no exception when it lays down the principle of individual responsibility in its declarations that, 'Whoever commits a sin only commits it against his own soul', and that, 'No one shall be burdened with the burden of another soul, and man is only rewarded for he [himself] strives for' (al-Nisā', 4:111 and al-Najm, 53:38-39 respectively).

ومن يكسب إثما فإنّما يكسبه على نفسه.

ألا تزر وازرة وزر أخرى وأن ليس للانسان إلا ما سعى.

Privileges of high office, including that of the head of state, presidency or parliament, do not provide any exception to or immunity from the general implementation of this principle. Moreover, the citizen's duty of obedience to a legitimate government is not an absolute one in that the citizen is entitled to dispute with the rulers when the latter fail to comply with the injunctions of the *Sharīʿah*. This is the subject of the Qur'ānic *āyah* that follows:

> O you who believe! Obey God and obey the Messenger and those in authority among you. Then if you dispute about a matter, refer it to God and to the Messenger. (al-Nisā', 4:59)

يا ايّها الّذين آمنوا أطيعوا اللّه وأطيعوا الرسول وأولى الأمر منكم
فإن تنازعتم في شيء فردّوه إلى اللّه والرسول.

Citizens are thus enjoined to obey rulers, but only if the rulers are themselves committed to the rules of *Sharīʿah*. While obedience remains the principal theme of this *āyah*, the latter portion of the text clearly allows disputation with rulers. The text also makes clear that both parties to such disputes, that is the ruler and the ruled, must submit to God's law as the final arbiter of their differences. It is further provided in a *ḥadīth*:

> A Muslim is under duty to listen and to obey in what he likes or dislikes unless he is commanded to commit a sin; when he is commanded to commit a sin, he is under no obligation to hear or obey.[3]

السمع والطاعة على المرء المسلم فيما احب وكره ما لم يؤمر بمعصية، فإن أمر بمعصية فلا سمع ولا طاعة.

Obedience is thus required in respect of responsible rulers who consider themselves accountable to God and to the community. If a command is found to be manifestly unlawful, the person to whom it is addressed is entitled to disobey it even if it is a military order, or any other order. The ruling of this *ḥadīth* is also in harmony with the essence of *ḥisbah* in that every individual is directly responsible for enjoining good and avoiding and forbidding what is manifestly unlawful.

The following *ḥadīth* also shows that no one is beyond accountability. Indeed everyone is accountable for what is placed under his charge:

> Be aware that each one of you is a guardian and responsible for that which is in his custody. The *imām* is a guardian and he is responsible for his subject; a man is a guardian and he is responsible for his family; a woman is the guardian of her husband's home and children and she is responsible for them [...] Surely, each one of you is a guardian and responsible for his charges.[4]

الا كلّكم راع وكلّكم مسؤول عن رعيته، فالامام الّذي على النّاس راع وهو مسؤول عن رعيته، والرجل راع على اهل بيته وهو مسؤول عن رعيته، والمرأة راعية على اهل بيت زوجها وولده وهي مسؤولة عنهم [...] الا كلّكم راع مسؤول عن رعيته.

Accountability has thus become a general principle that applies to everyone within and beyond the affairs of government. But since the reference to the *imām*/head of state occurs immediately after the general declaration of the *ḥadīth*, this becomes the most important area of accountability. The Prophet ﷺ also declared in another *ḥadīth*:

> No servant of God whom God has made custodian over others dies without this predicament: God will forbid the countenance of paradise to him

if he has died while betraying those who were in his custody.[5]

ما من عبد يسترعيه اللّه رعية يموت يوم يموت وهو غاش لرعيته إلا حرّم اللّه عليه الجنّة.

The citizen is strongly encouraged to be upright and assiduous in reminding the deviant ruler of his responsibility with sincerity and truth. Thus it is provided in another *ḥadīth* that 'the best form of *jihād* is to utter a word of truth to an oppressive ruler'.[6]

افضل الجهاد كلمة حق عند سلطان جائر

The basic message of this *ḥadīth* is confirmed in yet another *ḥadīth* stating that the one who turns a blind eye to injustice becomes in effect a party to it:

> When the people see an oppressor [committing acts of oppression] and they do not take him by the hand [to alert him], they come close to the point where God may extend the same punishment to all of them.[7]

انّ الناس اذا رأوا الظالم فلم يأخذوا على يديه اوشك من يعمّهم اللّه بعقاب منه.

The warning here is against injustice (*ẓulm*) which is *ḥarām* and must therefore be prevented, and no one should remain indifferent or silent when they see it being committed. It becomes a right therefore of everyone to alert others to it and to lodge a complaint about it to the authorities[8]

Accountability of government leaders to the people finds vivid expression in the precedent of the Rightly-Guided Caliphs. The first Caliph Abū Bakr went on record, for instance, by addressing the people, in his inaugural speech following his election to office, with the following words: 'O people! I have been entrusted with authority over you, but I am not the best of you. Assist me if I am right and rectify me when I am wrong.'[9] Abū Bakr's successor, ʿUmar ibn al-Khaṭṭāb, also asked the people, during his inaugural speech, to 'rectify any aberration' they might see in him. A man from the audience addressed the Caliph saying that, 'if we see deviation on your part, we shall rectify it by the sword'. The Caliph praised God that there was someone who would be so rigorously prepared to stand for righteousness.[10] This early precedent clearly acknowledged the citizen's freedom to criticise government leaders. The fact that Abū Bakr and ᶜUmar listened to people's criticism and responded to it is proven by historical evidence.[11] The Umayyad Caliph ᶜUmar ibn ᶜAbd al-ᶜAzīz (d. 101/720) has similarly been quoted to have said in an address to the people, 'I am one among you, except that God Most High has placed a greater burden on my shoulders.'[12]

NOTES

1. Muslim, *Mukhtaṣar Ṣaḥīḥ Muslim*, p. 16, *ḥadīth* no. 34.
2. Muslim, *Mukhtaṣar Ṣaḥīḥ Muslim, K. al-Imārah: b. Karāhiyyah al-Imārah Bi-ghayr Ḍarūrah.*
3. Muslim, *Mukhtaṣar Ṣaḥīḥ Muslim*, p. 322, *ḥadīth* no. 1226.
4. Al-Bukhārī, *Ṣaḥīḥ al-Bukhārī*, IX, *ḥadīth* 252.
5. Muslim, *Mukhtaṣar Ṣaḥīḥ Muslim*, p. 329, *ḥadīth* no. 1211
6. Ibn Mājah, *Sunan, K. al-Fitan, b. al-Amr bi'l-Maᶜrūf wa Nahy ᶜan al-Munkar, ḥadīth* no. 4011.
7. Abū Dāwūd, *Sunan Abū Dāwūd*, Eng. trans. Ahmad Hasan, 3 vols., Lahore, Ashraf Press, 1984, *K. al-Malāḥim*, b. no. 17.
8. Cf. Maḥmūd al-Khālidi, *Maᶜālim al-Khilāfah fi'l-Fikr al-Siyāsī al-Islāmī*, Beirut, Dār al-Jīl, 1404/1984, p. 190.
9. ᶜAbd al-Mālik ibn Hishām, *al-Sīrah al-Nabawiyyah*, 2 vols., Cairo, Muṣṭafā al-Bābī al-Ḥalabī, 1936, IV, 262; Saᶜdī Abū Ḥabīb, *Dirāsah fī Minhāj al-Islām al-Siyāsī*, Beirut, Mu'assasat al-Risālah, 1406/1985, p. 725.
10. Muḥammad Abū Zahrah, *al-Jarīmah wa'l-ᶜUqūbah fi'l-Fiqh al-Islāmī*, Cairo, Dār al-Fikhr al-ᶜArabī, n.d., p. 160; Muḥammad Fārūq al-Nabhān, *Niẓām al-Ḥukm fi'l-Islām*, Kuwait, Jāmiᶜat al-Kuwait, 1974, p. 250.
11. al-Sibāᶜī, *Ishtirākiyyāt*, p. 50.
12. Al-Sayyid Yāsīn, *al-Qaḍāyā al-Muᶜāṣirah wa'l-Khilāfah, Ḥiwār ᶜUlmānī Islāmī maᶜ al-Duktur Kamāl Abūl-Majd wa al-Shaykh Yūsuf al-Qaraḍāwī*, Cairo, Mirith li'l-Nashr wa'l-Maᶜlūmāt, 1999, p. 89.

CHAPTER TWELVE

Personal Privacy

The personal privacy of an individual is an integral part of his dignity, which is protected by the *Sharīʿah*. Privacy is a broad concept and the right to privacy refers not only to the sanctity of the home but to all aspects of privacy, such as that of personal correspondence, personal conversation, and personal financial affairs. Having said this, a certain degree of subjectivity is inherent in the concept of privacy. What is considered to be secret and confidential is to some extent a matter of personal opinion, just as it is also influenced by general custom, public opinion and culture. This might partially explain the absence of a comprehensive definition for the right of privacy. Even the notion of 'private dwelling' is not as clear-cut as might appear. Does 'private dwelling' signify a place with walls and barriers or not, and can the concept be extended to a car, boat, or premises in which one normally does not live? In principle, private dwelling is made immune to intrusion of all kinds. Strangers who wish to enter private homes are required to greet the inhabitants and make themselves known with courtesy and respect. The Qur'ān thus addresses the believers:

> Enter not houses other than your own until you have asked for permission and saluted their inmates [...] If you find no one therein, enter not until permission is given to you. If you are asked to go back, then go back. (al-Nūr, 24:27-29)

لا تدخلوا بيوتا غير بيوتكم حتى تستأنسوا وتسلّموا على أهلها
[...] فإن لم تجدوا فيها أحدا فلا تدخلوها حتى يؤذن لكم وإن
قيل لكم ارجعوا فارجعوا.

In fact, permission to enter a private home is to be solicited thrice, and if it is still not granted, the stranger should leave. This is clearly stated in a *ḥadīth* which informs the believers that, 'Asking for permission is [allowed up to] three times. If it is not granted to you, you must return.'[1]

الاستئذان ثلاث فإن أذن لك و إلا فارجع.

The *ḥadīth* here elaborates on the two requirements of familiarisation (*isti'nās*) and greeting (*taslīm*) that are laid down in the above-mentioned Qur'ānic *āyah*. The order of priority between these two requirements has also been specified in another *ḥadīth*, which simply declares that 'the Prophet ﷺ said: "Greeting precedes conversation"'.[2]

قال رسول اللّه صلى اللّه عليه وسلم السلام قبل الكلام.

Commentators have elaborated that 'uninhabited dwellings' in this *āyah* include, in addition to its obvious meaning, public places, shops, offices, guest-houses and hotels, which are normally open to visitors and permission to enter these is not a requirement.

It is also noted in the relevant commentaries that the requirement of *isti'dhān* represented a Qur'ānic reform as the Arab traditions had not taken a clear stand on this before. People often entered other people's dwellings without asking for permission or greeting the inhabitants. They simply declared themselves, after the entry, by such utterances as 'it is me' (*anā, anā*) or '*laqad dhakaltu*' ('I have come' or 'I have entered') and they did so regardless of the inconvenience they might cause to the inhabitants, in the event especially when the latter were not ready to receive visitors, or found a surprise visit particularly inconvenient.[3]

As for the question of whether threefold repetition of permission to enter is a requirement in every case, the *ᶜulamā'* have responded that it is not a requirement, and should the permission be granted upon the first request, there is no need for repetition. Repetition is not a part of the original injunction; it is a supplementary addition by the *Sunnah* that is indicative of emphasis on the basic right of privacy, and lays down the limit of when one is to stop reiterating one's request for permission to enter. It is further stated that repetition beyond this limit may annoy the inmate and compromise the integrity of his right of privacy.[4] There is, however, a variant view, attributed to Qatādah ibn Diʿāmah, to the effect that triple *isti'dhān* is the correct interpretation of the Qur'ānic term '*tasta'nisū*' (familiarise yourselves) and it is therefore a requirement in every case.[5] This is, however, a weak opinion and the majority position is preferable. This states that the repetition is only for the sake of perfection, and should be resorted to whenever appropriate, but is not a requirement as such. And lastly, notwithstanding the sequence of the Qur'ānic text to the contrary, it is deemed to be preferable to greet inmates first, and then ask them for permission to enter thereafter.[6]

The rules of *Sharīʿāh* concerning the privacy of the home may be extended by analogy to private cars, boats and caravans. These too are protected by the provisions that require permission and making oneself known prior to entry. These are not only protected by the general rules of the *Sharīʿah* relating to private property but also by the rules concerning the privacy of the home. The legal maxim of *fiqh* which proclaims that 'it is not permissible for anyone to interfere with the property of another without the latter's permission',[7] clearly protects the right of ownership. One who violates the private property of another may be guilty of theft or other property offences, and the specific rules of *Sharīʿah* will apply to the case. But even if one commits no property offence, such as burglary and theft, and merely violates the privacy of the house-owner and occupant by surreptitious and unsolicited search for information, one will have violated the owner's right of privacy.

Spying (*tajassus*) is forbidden by the clear text of the Qur'ān, and so is indulgence in suspicion and surreptitious activities that are degrading and offensive to the personal dignity of the individual (al-Ḥujurāt, 49:12). The Qur'ānic prohibition on spying occurs in absolute and unqualified terms (i.e. *wa lā tajassasū*), which means that it is totally proscribed, regardless of the purpose that might be served by it. The verse is also addressed to everyone, including government agencies and the *muḥtasib*, that is the officer in charge of *ḥisbah*, who is not permitted to use espionage as a means of promoting *ḥisbah* (i.e. commanding good and forbidding evil). The *muḥtasib* must act on the basis of what he knows through direct observation, without recourse to espionage, evesdropping or other methods of searching for evidence.[8] The second Caliph, ʿUmar ibn al-Khaṭṭāb, clarified the official position when he said that the government acts on what is evident; one who exhibits good character should not be suspected of anything but good; for the inner secrets of people are only known to God Most High.[9] The general text of the Qur'ān on the prohibition of spying similarly means that all varieties of espionage are included. Furthermore the Qur'ānic text on spying is immediately preceded by an address to the believers to 'avoid indulgence in suspicion, for surely suspicion in most cases is sinful, and spy not' (al-Ḥujurāt, 49:12).

يا أيها الذين أمنوا اجتنبوا كثيرا من الظن إنّ بعض الظن إثم.

Spying originates in suspicion, which is also to be avoided as far as possible, even though the wording of the text is not as categorical on suspicion as it is on spying. The text here seems to permit suspicion that is based on reasonable grounds. The point, however, is that both are seen as a threat to personal dignity, and a violation of the individual's right to privacy. The prohibition of spying also includes the opening of personal letters and confidential correspondence. This is, in fact, the subject of a *ḥadīth* to the effect that, 'One who looks into the letter of his brother without his permission, is like looking into the fire of Hell.'[10]

من نظر في كتاب اخيه بغير اذنه فانما ينظر في النار.

The prohibition on spying is thus addressed to everyone and to all concerned, including law enforcement agencies, individuals and government leaders.

The *Sunnah* is equally emphatic on the subject of unfounded suspicion, which is seen to be the starting point of spying. The Prophet ﷺ has thus warned people to:

> Beware of suspicion, for suspicion may be totally untrue and may amount to the worst form of lying; and do not spy on one another and do not expose each other's hidden failings.[11]

اياكم والظنّ فإنّ الظنّ الكذب الحديث ولا تجسّوا ولا تعيروا.

Suspicion that originates in malice and has no evidential basis is not to be pursued, and the best advice is to abandon it altogether. The latitude that is shown in this way ranks in merit as an act of worship, as the following *ḥadīth* simply proclaims: 'Thinking well [of others] partakes of worship.'[12]

حسن الظنّ من العبادة.

Commenting on this and the preceding *ḥadīth*, al-Jundī noted that the reference is to suspicion based on mere doubt, and pursuing it any further means attaching value to it, which the *ḥadīth* has clearly advised against.[13]

Another theme related to personal privacy is *satr al-ʿawrāt*, literally concealing the nakedness of others. This is one of the major themes of the *Sunnah* and the instruction that the Prophet ﷺ has given on it is forceful in that it is not confined to moral guidance, but also involves legal action. The jurists have understood much of the *Sunnah* on this subject to be of legal import and have therefore advanced their juristic conclusion relating to spying accordingly. Our review of some of the leading *ḥadīth* underscores the virtue of hiding other people's weaknesses:

> He who conceals the nakedness of a Muslim, God will conceal his nakedness both in this world and the Hereafter.[14]

من ستر مسلما ستره اللّه في الدنيا والآخرة

Another version of the same *ḥadīth* has it that, 'One who conceals the hidden failings of others does not fail to enjoy God's forbearance over his failings on the Day of Judgement.'[15]

لا يستر عبد عبدا في الدنيا إلا ستره اللّه يوم القيامة.

It is further provided in another *ḥadīth*:

> Do not annoy your fellow Muslims; do not impute evil to them, and do not uncover their nakedness. For behold, anyone who exposes the nakedness of his Muslim brother, God will expose his nakedness.[16]

لا تؤذوا المسلمين ولاتعيروا، ولا تتبعوا عوراتهم، فانّ من يتبع عورة اخيه المسلم يتبع اللّه عورته.

The Prophet ﷺ has clearly declared exposing the hidden failing of a fellow Muslim to be antithetical to the fraternity and affection that Islam consistently emphasises. The same attitude seems to have been encouraged with regard to non-Muslims, as we read in another *ḥadīth*: 'If you try to expose the nakedness of the people, you are likely to spread corruption among them.'[17]

انّك إن اتبعت عورات النّاس افسدتهم او كدت ان تفسدهم.

The general language of this *ḥadīth* and the reference it makes to people at large tend to confirm that it is addressed to Muslims and non-Muslims alike.

NOTES

1. Muslim, *Mukhtaṣar Ṣaḥīḥ Muslim*, *ḥadīth* no. 1421.
2. Muḥammad ᶜAbd al-Raḥmān al-Mubārakfūrī, *Tuḥfat al-Ahwāzī Sharḥ Jāmiᶜ al-Tirmidhī*, ed. ᶜAbd al-Raḥmān Uthmān, 3rd edn, Beirut, Dār al-Fikr, 1239/1979, IX, 170.
3. Cf. Abū Dāwūd, *Mukhtaṣar Sunan Abī Dāwūd, K. al-Adab, b. al-rajul yasta'dhinu bi'l-daqq, ḥadīth* no. 5187.
4. Al-Alūsī, *Rūḥ al-Maᶜānī*, XVIII, 135; Ḥusnī al-Jundī, *Ḍamānāt Ḥurmat al-Ḥayāt al-Khāṣṣah fi'l-Islām*, Cairo, Dār al-Naḥdah al-ᶜArabiyyah, 1413/1993, p. 87.
5. Al-Ḥāfiẓ Ibn Kathīr, *Tafsīr al-Qur'ān al-ᶜAẓīm* (also known as *Tafsīr Ibn Kathīr*), 4 vols, Cairo, Dār al-Shaᶜb, 1393/1973, III, 282.
6. Ibn Qayyim al-Jawziyyah, *Zād al-Maᶜād fi Hudā Khayr al-ᶜIbād*, Mecca, al-Maṭbaᶜah al-Makkiyyah, n.d, II, 430.
7. Al-Dughmī, *Ḥimāyat* p. 123.
8. Muḥammad Rākān al-Dughmī, *al-Tajassus wa Aḥkāmuhu fi'l- al-Ḥayāt al-Khāṣṣah fi'l-Sharīᶜah al-Islāmiyyah*, 2nd edn, Cairo, Dār al-Salām li'l-Ṭibāᶜah wa'l-Nashr, 1406/1986, p. 149.
9. Al-Ṭabarī, *Ta'rīkh*, V, 26.
10. Al-Suyūṭī, *al-Jāmiᶜ al-Ṣaghir*, p. 165; al-Maqdisī, *al-Ādāb al-Sharᶜiyyah*, II, 166.
11. Muslim, *Ṣaḥīḥ Muslim, Kitāb al-Birr wa'l-Ṣillah, Bāb al-Nahy ᶜan al-Tajassus*.
12. Abū Dāwūd, *Sunan Abū Dāwūd, Kitāb al-Adab, Bāb fi Ḥusn al-Ẓann*.
13. al-Jundī, *Ḍamānāt*, p. 172.

14. Abū Dāwūd, *Mukhtaṣar Sunan Abī Dāwūd, Kitāb al-Adab b. al-Mu'akhat*
15. Muslim, *Mukhtaṣar Ṣaḥīḥ Muslim*, p. 473, *ḥadīth* no. 1777.
16. Al-Tirmidhī, *Sunan al-Tirmidhī*, III, 255, *Kitāb al-Birr*, *ḥadīth* no. 84.
17. Abū Dāwūd, *Mukhtaṣar Sunan Abī Dāwūd, Kitāb al-Adab*, *b. al-Nahy ʿan al-Tajassus*.

CHAPTER THIRTEEN

Compassion and Tolerance

The Prophet ﷺ characterised Islam as *dīn al-samāḥah*, or a religion of tolerance, which he manifested in his own lifestyle, and he also advised others to be easy going and tolerant. He strongly discouraged extremism and excess in all matters, especially in religious ones, and warned his followers against it as follows:

> Avoid extremism, for people have been led to destruction because of extremism.[1]

عليكم بالغلوّ فإنّما هلكوا من قبلكم في الغلوّ.

The Qur'ān also characterises Islam as an upright (*ḥanīf*) faith, which is to maintain a correct fusion of values that is harmonious with sound reason and an enlightened nature: 'And set your face toward the religion, upright, and never in any way be of the unbelievers' (Yūnus, 10:105). *Ḥanīfiyyah* and *samāḥah* are often treated as complementary to one another, and are often used together to describe Islam. The Qur'ān also uses '*ḥanīfan musliman*' in reference to prophet Abraham (Āl ʿImrān, 3:67) who was an upright and unflinching monotheist. Islam is also characterised as a religion of nature (*dīn al-fiṭrah*), a religion which is compatible with the enlightened nature and conscience of human beings, neither inclining to one extreme nor another, and it appeals to the best side of human nature (al-Rūm, 30:30). The prophet ﷺ is reported to have said: 'May the mercy of God be on one who is lenient when he sells, lenient when he buys, and lenient when he makes a demand.'[2]

رحم اللّه عبدا سمحا اذا باع، سمحا اذا اشترى، سمحا اذا اقتضى.

The tolerant outlook of Islam is further manifested in the Qur'ānic directive to 'take to forgiveness, enjoin good, and turn away from the ignorant' (al-Aʿrāf, 7:199).

خذ العفو وأمر بالعرف وأعرض عن الجاهلين.

The Qur'ān here encourages the believers to incline towards forgiveness and not be eager to take issue with all and sundry, but show tolerance with what emanates from ignorance rather than malice. The Prophet ﷺ has added his voice to this and spoken of leniency and compassion on numerous occasions. Abū Zahrah has quoted the following *ḥadīth* on the subjects of leniency and compassion (*raḥmah* and *rifq*):

> One who forbids leniency closes the door to all goodness.

من يحرّم الرفق يحرّم الخير كلّه.

> God shows mercy to the merciful servants. Be merciful to the inhabitants of the earth and He who is in heaven will be merciful to you.

الراحمون يرحمهم الرحمان، ارحموا من في الارض يرحمكم من في السماء.

> Mercy is not denied to anyone except to those who are cruel to others.

لا تنزع الرحمة إلا من شقى.

> One who is not compassionate, God will not be compassionate to him.[3]

من لا يرحم لا يرحم.

On occasions, when the Prophet ﷺ assigned government duties to officials, he would instruct them to 'give good news [to the people] and do not turn them away, and facilitate [people's affairs] rather than making them difficult'.

بشروا ولا تنفروا ويسروا ولاتعسروا.

A prominent figure among the Companions, Abū Mūsā al-Ashʿarī, told the Prophet ﷺ: 'You remind us so frequently concerning *raḥmah* even though we actually think that we are compassionate toward one another', to which the Prophet replied: 'But I mean *raḥmah* to all [*innamā urīd al-raḥmah bi'l-kāffah*]',[4] which means to humanity at large, not just to humans alone, but also to animals and to all of God creatures.

According to another report, when the Prophet ﷺ learned that the Quraysh of Mecca were experiencing drought, he sent Ḥātab ibn Abī Baltaʿah to Abū Sufyān, the leader of Mecca, with five hundred dinars to purchase wheat for distribution among the poor. This he did inspite of the then prevailing state of war between Muslims and the Quraysh of Mecca.[5]

ʿĀ'ishah reported that the Prophet ﷺ was always inclined towards preventing hardship and to lightening the people's burden as far as was possible. Her report thus provides that:

> The Prophet did not choose but the easier of two alternatives unless it amounted to sin.[6]

ما اختار بين امرين إلا ايسرهما مالم يكن اثما.

Islam therefore advises against unnecessary rigour in the enforcement of its laws. The Qur'ān has made it clear on more than one occasion that 'God intends every facility for you and He does not intend to put you in hardship' (al-Baqarah, 2:185; see also al-Ḥajj, 22:78).

يريد الله بكم اليسر ولا يريد بكم العسر.

The Prophet ﷺ reiterated the spirit of this declaration in another *ḥadīth* in which he advised people to take advantage of the concessions and easier choices that God Most High has made available for

His servants. Hence the *ḥadīth* that:

> God loves to see that His concessions are utilised, just as He loves to see that His commandments are obeyed.[7]

إنّ اللّه يحبّ ان تؤتى رخصه كما يحبّ ان تؤتى عزائمه.

The Prophet ﷺ condemned hair-splitting searches and extreme positions on issues that stemmed from suspicion and over-indulgence in negative thinking. His instruction on this point simply repeats the destructive consequences of *tanaṭṭu*ᶜ:

> Perished are the hair-splitters, perished are the hair-splitters, perished are the hair-splitters.[8]

هلك المتنطعون، هلك المتنطعون، هلك المتنطعون.

A juristic conclusion drawn from these guidelines is that since bringing ease and preventing hardship for the people is a purpose and objective that God Most High and His Messenger ﷺ have chosen and upheld, it is not permissible for a *muftī*, judge or *mujtahid* to opt for harsher choices and difficult solutions in cases where easier alternatives can equally be applied.

Moderating justice (*ᶜadl*) with equity (*iḥsān*) may be said to be another aspect of tolerance in Islam. Justice and equity tend to moderate one another in many situations, for example where a strict application of the rules of justice leads to rigidity and hardship, in which case recourse may be made to the rules of equity (*istiḥsān*). *Qiṣāṣ*, or just retaliation, for example, is a *Sharīᶜah* principle that is designed to obtain justice. Yet the Qur'ān also advises forgiveness by way of *iḥsān* in situations where compassion rather than strict enforcement of *qiṣāṣ* may be appropriate.

The Prophet ﷺ expressed his vision of Medinan society by emphasising mutual kindness and affection among the believers, as stated in the following *ḥadīth*:

> The believers, in their love, mutual kindness and close ties are like one body; when any part complains, the whole body responds to it with wakefulness and fever.[9]

مثل المؤمنين في توادهم و تراحمهم وتعاطفهم كمثل الجسد الواحد. اذا اشتكى منه عضوا تداعى له سائر الجسد بالسهر والحمى.

The Prophet ﷺ reiterated the same message when he said: 'None of you truly believes until he wishes for his brother that which he wishes for himself.'[10]

لا يؤمن احدكم حتى يحبّ لا خيه ما يحبّ لنفسه.

In sum, Islam is emphatic on compassion (*raḥmah*), forgiveness (*ᶜafw*), and fraternity (*ukhūwwah*) within the community of Muslims and the wider context of human relations generally. I may mention in passing again what I have earlier said, namely that two of the most favoured of God's ninety-nine most beautiful names (*al-asmā' al-ḥusnā*) are al-Raḥmān and al-Raḥīm (Most Compassionate, Most Merciful.) God's illustrious attributes and names thus set the ideals of human behaviour that are to be emulated and followed. Tolerance and *raḥmah* as such become the most favoured of all attributes and they become characteristic of Islam itself.

NOTES

1. Ibn Ḥanbal, *Musnad Ibn Ḥanbal*, vol. V, *ḥadīth* no. 3655.
2. Al-ᶜAsqalānī, *Jawāhir Ṣaḥīḥ al-Bukhārī*, *ḥadīth* no. 275.
3. Abū Zahrah, *al-Mujtamaᶜ al-Insānī*, pp. 57-58; Many of these *ḥadīth* also appear in al-Bukhārī, *Ṣaḥīḥ al-Bukhārī, Kitāb al-Adab, Bāb Rahmat an-Nās wa'l-Bahā'im*. See also al-Nawawī, *Riyāḍ al-Ṣaliḥīn*, p. 113, *ḥadīth* no. 118.
4. Abū Zahrah, *al-Mujtamaᶜ al-Insānī*, p. 58.
5. Ibid.
6. Muslim, *Mukhtaṣar Ṣaḥīḥ Muslim*, p. 412, *ḥadīth* no. 1546.
7. Ibn Qayyim, *Iᶜlām al-Muwaqqiᶜīn ᶜan rabb al-ᶜĀlamīn*, ed. Muḥammad Munīr al-Dimashqī, Cairo, Idārat al-Ṭibāᶜah al-Munīriyyah, n.d., II, p. 242.
8. Muslim, *Mukhtaṣar Ṣaḥīḥ Muslim*, p. 481, *ḥadīth* no. 1824.
9. Ibid., p. 472, *ḥadīth* no. 1774.
10. Al-Nawawī, *Riyāḍ al-Ṣaliḥīn*, p. 113, *ḥadīth* no. 118.

CHAPTER FOURTEEN

Social Decorum

One of the major themes of Islam's teaching in the sphere of social behaviour is *ḥusn al-khulq,* that is, pleasant behaviour and dignified social encounter. *Ḥusn al-khulq* is a comprehensive term that may be said to consist of three component parts relating firstly to thought and intention; secondly to speech and conduct; and thirdly to honouring certain individuals and personalities in particular. The Prophet ﷺ has declared in a *ḥadīth* that 'the best part of faith is to possess beautiful manners'[1]

أفضل الإيمان خلق حسن.

and he said in another *ḥadīth* that 'I have been sent in order to perfect moral virtues [in you].'[2]

بعثت لأتمم مكارم الأخلاق.

The Prophet ﷺ is also reported to have said that 'the essence of virtue is manifested in good behaviour, whereas sinful conduct is that which makes you feel uncomfortable, and you yourself dislike others knowing about it'.[3]

البر حسن الخلق و الإثم ما حاك في نفسك و كرهت أن يطلع عليه الناس.

The Prophet ﷺ here describes some of the qualities of *ḥusn al-khulq* and the impact it has, for otherwise the concept is so broad that it does not easily lend itself to comprehensive definition. It would appear that the personal judgement and conscience of the individual involved is the foremost indicator of *ḥusn al-khulq*. Thus it is implied that if one feels unhappy about one's own conduct, one is likely to have behaved contrary to *ḥusn al-khulq*.

At the level of thought and intention, Islam nurtures good will and benevolence towards others and avoidance of suspicion concerning them. The Qur'ān thus enjoins the believers to 'beware of suspicion, for suspicion in some cases partakes of sin' (al-Ḥujurāt, 49:12).

يا أيها الذين أمنوا اجتنبوا كثيرا من الظن إنّ بعض الظن إثم.

Suspicion is permitted only when it is founded on a reasonable cause, when, for instance, the police observe an individual in suspicious circumstances and decide to question him; this would not merely be a case of suspicion *in abstracto* but one grounded in reality. This kind of suspicion is often referred to as *al-ẓann al-mubāḥ* (permissible suspicion), which may lead to the discovery of truth. The substance of this teaching is taken a step further in a *ḥadīth* that advises the avoidance of all suspicion: 'Beware of suspicion, for suspicion may be totally untrue and may amount to the worst form of lying, and do not spy.'[4]

إياكم والظن فإن الظن أكذب الحديث ولا تجسسوا.

The Prophet ﷺ has moreover instructed the believers to 'avoid engaging in hatred, jealousy, and speaking ill behind the back of one another'.[5]

لا تباغضوا ولا تحاسدوا ولا تدابروا.

In yet another *ḥadīth* the Prophet ﷺ stressed the value of good will when he said: 'Acts are to be judged by the intention behind them. Every man deserves what he deserves according to his intention.'[6]

إنما الأعمال بالنيات وإنما لكل أمرئ ما نوى.

Speech is undoubtedly the focus of Islam's teachings on *ḥusn al-khulq*, and it is also the *locus* where dignified social encounter acquires much of its meaning. The Qur'ān emphasises moderation and justice in speech and then directs everyone to try to be pleasant and say what is good and positive. Of the relevant passages of the Qur'ān, attention may be drawn to the following:

And when you speak, speak with justice. (al-Anʿām, 6:152)

واذا قلتم فاعدلوا.

O you who believe, fear God and say a word in pursuit of righteousness. (al-Aḥzāb, 33:70)

يا أيها الذين أمنوا التقوا اللّه وقولوا قولاً سديدا.

And speak to people with courtesy and rectitude. (al-Baqarah, 2:83)

وقولوا للناس حسنا.

And tell my servants to say that which is best. (al-Isrā', 17:53)

وقل لعبادي يقول التي هي أحسن.

The Prophet ﷺ has taken the substance of these teachings a step further by declaring that well-intended and dignified speech is reflective of the firmness of one's faith. This is the subject of the following two *ḥadīth*:

Whoever believes in God and the Last Day, let him speak when he has something good to say, or else remain silent.[7]

من كان يؤمن باللّه واليوم الآخر فليقل خيرا أو ليصمت.

A sign of the piety of a Muslim is to remain silent regarding that which does not concern him.[8]

من حسن إسلام المرء تركه مالا يعنيه.

In yet another *ḥadīth*, the Prophet ﷺ has drawn a parallel between pleasant speech and charity. Speech is a kind of charity, in other words, that everyone can afford to give. The *ḥadīth* simply declares that 'pleasant speech is a form of charity'.[9]

الكلمة الطيبة صدقة.

Even when one hears or sees misguided speech or conduct on the part of another person, Islam's advice is that one should not be easily swayed by it and let good will work its way first. This is the subject of the following Qur'ānic *āyah*:

Good deeds and evil ones can never be equal. Repel evil with what is better, then you will find that the one with whom you might have had enmity will become as though he were and intimate friend. (Fuṣṣilāt, 41:34)

ولا تستوى الحسنة ولا السيئة ادفع بالتى هي أحسن فإذا الّذى
بينك و بينه عداوة كأنه ولي حميم.

Evil speech and conduct should not, in other words, be reciprocated in kind. To show the kind of latitude that the Qur'ān advises here, in appropriate places, would work like a powerful agent for creating good relations, even friendship between people.

One of the major guidelines of the *Sharīʿah* toward social decorum and creating a pleasant social atmosphere is that people should restrain themselves from *al-jahr bi'l-sū' min al-qawl*, that is, the public utterance of harmful words. Thus the Qur'ān declares:

God loves not the public utterance of harmful words except by one who has been wronged. God is ever Hearer and All-knowing. If you do good openly or keep it secret, or forgive evil, rest assured that God is forgiving and All-powerful. (al-Nisā', 4:148-149)

لا يحبّ اللّه الجهر بالسوء من القول إلا من ظلم و كان اللّه سميعا عليما إن تبدوا خيرا أو تخفوه أو تعفوا عن سوء فإن اللّه كان عفوّاً قديرا.

The message clearly is that God rewards self-restraint and patience in the face of adversity and evil. The public utterance of harmful words is a broad Qur'ānic concept that can apply to all varieties of speech, writing and other forms of expression that threaten to mar an atmosphere of fraternity and peace in society, and violates social dignity and decorum. Only one exception is made to this, which is in respect to injustice so that the cry of the oppressed may be heard and attended to. The substance of the Qur'ānic address above is upheld in at least two *ḥadīth*, one of which declares that 'a Muslim is one from whose tongue and hand other Muslims are safe'.[10]

المسلم من سلم المسلمون من لسانه و يده.

In another *ḥadīth* the Prophet ﷺ declares, 'The whole of my *ummah* is forgiven except for those who declare in public [and boast about] the evil they have committed.'[11]

كل أمتى معافى إلا المجاهرين.

'*Mujāhirīn*' in this *ḥadīth* refers to individuals who commit evil in privacy, at night time, or away from the public eye, and then, instead of trying to make up for it or ask for forgiveness, they actually broadcast and declare the fact, thereby violating the requirements of self-restraint and social decorum.

The Qur'ānic guidelines on disputation and dialogue in religious matters, including the call to religion, or *daʿwah,* is that it must be conducted in the most eloquent and reasonable manner possible. Thus with reference to *daʿwah,* Muslims are enjoined to observe the following guidelines:

> And argue with them [the disbelievers] in the best manner. (al-Naḥl, 16:125)

وجادلهم بالتى هى أحسن.

And argue not with the People of the Book except in the best manner. (al-ʿAnkabūt, 29:46)

ولا تجادلوا أهل الكتاب إلا بالتي هي أحسن.

This is also general advice to everyone, so that when Muslims engage in arguments among themselves, they must be reasonable, pleasant and courteous. Thus according to another Qur'ānic directive:

And guide others to be [pleasant and] righteous in speech and lead them to the path of the Praised. (al-Ḥajj, 22:24)

وهدوا إلى الطيب من القول وهدوا إلى صراط الحميد.

The social implications of this address are clear in that the text not only requires that one should be pleasant in manner and speech but that one should set a good example to guide and persuade others to do the same.

The third requirement of social decorum in Islam is manifested, more specifically, in its teaching concerning the treatment of certain individuals and personalities within and outside the family. Honouring one's parents is a textual requirement that is the subject of a number of Qur'ānic directives, which are discussed in the context of *takāful* (social support) below. Other persons whom the Qur'ān and *Sunnah* recommend one to treat with dignity and decorum are the pious and learned, especially in the religious sciences, one's neighbours, and one's guests. More generally, however, the *Sunnah* has declared exchange of greetings (*salām*), responding to invitations, visiting the sick, the offering of sincere advice (*naṣīḥah*), and escorting one's funeral to be among the rights that all Muslims have over one another.[12] The Qur'ān clearly speaks in praise of the learned when it declares that 'God will raise by degrees those of you who believe and possess knowledge' (al-Mujādilah, 58:11).

يرفع اللّه الذين آمنوا منكم والذين أوتوا العلم درجات.

The Prophet ﷺ is also reported to have said, 'The best of you are those who learn the Qur'ān and those who teach it.'[13]

خيركم من تعلم القرآن وعلّمه.

It is then stated in another *ḥadīth* that 'God means a person well when He helps him to gain knowledge of the religion'.[14]

من يريد اللّه به خيرا ليفقهه في الدين.

Honouring one's neighbours and guests is the subject of several *ḥadīth*, one of which provides: 'Anyone who has faith in God and in the Last Day—let him be good to his neighbour; anyone who has faith in God and the Last Day—let him honour his guest; and anyone who has faith in God and the Last Day—let him say something good or else remain silent.'[15]

من كان يؤمن باللّه واليوم الآخر فليحسن إلى جاره ومن كان يؤمن باللّه واليوم الآخر فليكرم ضيفه، ومن كان يؤمن باللّه واليوم الآخر فليقل خيرا أو ليسكت.

The Qur'ān enjoins courteous treatment and kindness (*iḥsān*) to the neighbour-cum-relative, the neighbour who is not a relative, and a companion on a journey (al-Nisā', 4:36). A rule of courtesy laid down in the *Sunnah* concerning neighbours and companions is that, 'If there be three of you in each other's company, the two of you should not confide in one another while isolating the other, as this may dismay the latter—until you mingle with the people [i.e. others join you].'[16]

إذا كنتم ثلاثة فلا يتناجى اثنان دون الآخر حتى تختلطوا بالناس من أجل أن يحزنه.

The Prophet ﷺ is also reported to have said that 'Gabriel continued to commend the neighbour to me till I almost thought he was going to assign him a share in inheritance'.[17]

ما زال جبريل يوصيني بالجار حتى ظننت أنه ليورثه.

NOTES

1. Al-Tabrīzī, *Mishkāt*, vol. I, *ḥadīth* no. 46.
2. Ibid., vol. III, *ḥadīth* no. 5097.
3. Muslim, *Mukhtaṣar Ṣaḥīḥ Muslim*, p. 476, *ḥadīth* no. 1794.
4. Ibid., p. 477, *ḥadīth* no. 1803.
5. Ibid, p. 477, *ḥadīth* no. 1800.
6. Ibid, p. 287, *ḥadīth* no. 1080.
7. Ibid, p. 218, *ḥadīth* no. 844.
8. Al-Tabrīzī, *Mishkāt*, vol. III, *ḥadīth* no. 4839.
9. Al-Nawawī, *Riyāḍ al-Ṣāliḥīn*, p. 284, *ḥadīth* no. 699.
10. Muslim, *Mukhtaṣar Ṣaḥīḥ Muslim*, p. 23, *ḥadīth* no. 69.
11. Ibid., p. 216, *ḥadīth* no. 832.
12. Ibid., p. 374, *ḥadīth* no. 1418.
13. Al-Tabrīzī, *Mishkāt*, vol. I, *ḥadīth* no. 2109.
14. Ibid., *ḥadīth* no. 200.
15. Muslim, *Mukhtaṣar Ṣaḥīḥ Muslim*, p. 16, *ḥadīth* no. 32.
16. Ibid., p. 376, *ḥadīth* no. 1340.
17. Ibid., p. 474, *ḥadīth* no. 1780.

CHAPTER FIFTEEN

Safeguards against Physical Abuse

Physical abuse and aggression are entirely forbidden by the *Sharīᶜah*, and no one, including government leaders and judges, are allowed to punish unless it is in the cause of justice. Punishment compromises personal dignity in most cases, but especially so when it is unjustified and oppressive. The Qur'ānic mandate on this is conveyed in broad and all-encompassing terms when it proclaims that 'there shall be no hostility except against the oppressors' (al-Baqarah, 2:193).

فلا عدوان إلا على الظالمين.

This is endorsed in a *ḥadīth* which declares in equally broad and unqualified terms that 'God will punish [in the Hereafter] those who punish people in this world'.[1]

إن اللّه يعذب الذين يعذبون الناس في الدنيا.

In yet another *ḥadīth* it is provided that 'the back of a Muslim [i.e. his body] is immune [from harm] unless it be in the cause of justice'.[2]

ظهر المسلم حمى إلا بحقه.

The Prophet ﷺ is also reported to have said that 'the one who slaps the faces of others does not belong to us'.[3]

ليس منا من ضرب الخدود.

The Prophet also addressed the people in his Farewell Sermon (*khuṭbat al-widāʿ*) as follows: 'Just as this day of yours and this month of yours and this land of yours are sacred [must not be transgressed], so among you are your lives, your properties and your honour'.[4]

إن دماؤكم و أموالكم وأعراضكم بينكم حرام عليكم كحرمة يومكم هذا في شهركم هذا في بلدكم هذا.

The Qur'ān forbids all forms of aggression and directs the believers to 'avoid aggression, for God loves not the aggressors' (al-Baqarah, 2:190).

ولا تعتدوا إن اللّه لا يحب المعتدين.

The substance of this directive is upheld in a *ḥadīth* that provides, in an address to the believers: 'Do not intimidate a Muslim, for intimidating a Muslim is a grave transgression.'[5]

لا تروعوا المسلم فإن روعة المسلم ظلم عظيم.

According to another *ḥadīth*, the Prophet ﷺ said to his community:

> Do not annoy the Muslims, or defame them, and do not expose their nakedness. For one who exposes the nakedness of his Muslim brother, God will expose his own nakedness.[6]

لا تؤذوا المسلمين ولا تعيروا ولا تتبعوا عوراتهم، فإن من يتبع عورة أخيه المسلم يتبع اللّه عورته.

Punishment must not exceed the limits of moderation and appropriacy, as the Qur'ān directs in the following two verses:

> Whoever is aggressive towards you, your response must be proportionate to the aggression that was inflicted on you. (al-Baqarah, 2:194)

ومن اعتدى عليكم فاعتدوا عليه بمثل ما اعتدى عليكم.

> And if you decide to punish, then punish with the like of that with which you were afflicted, but yet if you show patience, it is certainly best for those who remain patient. (al-Naḥl, 16:126)

وإن عاقبتم فعاقبوا بمثل ما عوقبتم به ولئن صبرتم لهو خير للصابرين.

The Qur'ānic rule of reciprocity in punishment has, once again, been tempered by its recommendation of patience and self-restraint. One must not be rash in the application of penalties but show latitude and allow time for forgiveness and reform. This dignified approach to law enforcement is also reflected in the *ḥadīth* that directs the authorities to 'suspend the *ḥudūd* punishments in cases of doubt as far as you can. For it is better to err in forgiveness than to make an error in punishment'.[7]

ادرؤوا الحدود بالشبهات ما استطعتم، والخطاء في العفو خير من الخطاء في العقوبة.

The Prophet ﷺ has also given the following general instruction:

> When any of you fights, avoid striking [your opponents] on the face and do not strike the vital organs. [8]

اذا قاتل احدكم فليتق الوجه ولا يضرب مقاتله

When the Prophet ﷺ sent two of his leading Companions, Abū Mūsā al-Ashʿarī and Muʿādh ibn Jabal, as judges to the Yemen, he gave them the following instructions: 'Bring ease [to the people], not hardship, and give them good news, not gloom [that will repel them].'[9]

يسرا ولا تعسرا وبشرا ولا تنفرا.

According to another report, the Prophet ﷺ also said on that occasion: 'You have been sent in order to make things easy, not to make them difficult.'[10]

إنما بعثتم ميسرين ولم تبعثوا معسرين.

In yet another *ḥadīth*, the Prophet ﷺ declared:

> Leniency does not fail to yield beauty, and harshness does not fail to yield ugliness.[11]

الرفق لا يكون في شئ إلا زانه ولا ينزع من شئ إلا شانه.

Information on the precedent of the early Caliphs suggests that they conformed to the substance of these guidelines. It is thus reported that during the time of the second Caliph ᶜUmar ibn al-Khaṭṭāb, a soldier complained to the Caliph against one of the governors, Abū Mūsā al-Ashᶜarī, for having beaten him and shaven his hair due to a protest he had made over the portion he was given in the war booties. The Caliph wrote to al-Ashᶜarī and directed him as follows: if you did this in front of other people, then you must allow the plaintiff to retaliate in the same fashion, but if you did so quietly, let him also retaliate likewise. Al-Ashᶜarī asked the man to retaliate but then the man forgave him.[12]

A similar incident is reported with regard to ᶜAmr ibn al-ᶜĀṣ, who was governor of Egypt during the time of ᶜUmar ibn al-Khaṭṭāb. The governor's son had beaten someone for no good reason; the Caliph investigated the matter and when it turned out that the governor had over-stepped the limits, he was warned in these words: 'Since when have you enslaved people whom their mothers gave birth to as free individuals?'[13] The point was, of course, that people are born free. Freedom is a birth right that no one is entitled to derogate or take away, nor should anyone humiliate and abuse another person without just cause.

The *Sharīᶜah* also forbids violence to oneself, which is why suicide is forbidden, as is clear from the following Qur'ānic directive: 'And kill not yourselves, for God is Merciful to you' (al-Nisā', 4:29).

ولا تقتلوا أنفسكم إن الله كان بكم رحيما.

For those who commit the final act of aggression against themselves are the ones who are overwhelmed by having despaired of God's mercy. Just as taking one's own life is prohibited, so is inflicting injury on oneself and mutilation of parts of one's body, acts which make the perpetrator liable to a *ta*ᶜ*zīr* (deterrent) punishment.[14] There is also evidence in the Qur'ān (al-Nisā', 4:97) that subjecting oneself to indignity and oppression is not permissible.

The Prophet ﷺ also encouraged people to lead a healthy lifestyle when he declared that 'a believer who is strong [and healthy] is better and clearer to God than one who is weak but there is goodness in all of them'.[15]

المؤمن القوي خير وأحب الى اللّه من المؤمن الضعيف، وفي كل خير.

To those who suffer from ill-health, the Prophet ﷺ gave the following advice:

> Take care of your health, and seek a cure for any illness you might have, O servants of God! For God Most High has not created an infirmity without creating a cure for it, except for old age.[16]

تداووا عباد اللّه، فإن اللّه تعالى لم يضع داء إلا وضع له دواء غير داء واحد الهرم.

A careless attitude clearly cannot be condoned in the face of adversity and disease. The Qur'ān has directed the believers in no uncertain terms 'not to throw yourselves into the mouth of danger by your own hands' (al-Baqarah, 2:195).

ولا تلقوا بأيديكم إلى التهلكة.

Everyone is thus advised to exercise rational judgment in regard to bodily health and not, as it were, to expect miracles when this rational judgment is not followed. The Prophet ﷺ has given clear instruction to the believers as to what to do in the event of the breakout of a contagious disease:

When you hear that a plague has broken out in a place, and you are outside it, do not go there, but if the plague breaks out in a place where you are located, then do not leave or try to escape.[17]

إذا سمعتم بالوباء بأرض فلا تقدموا عليه، واذا وقع بأرض وأنتم بها فلا تخرجوا فراراً منه.

Cleanliness is greatly emphasised in Islam, so much so that it is declared an integral part of the Muslim faith: '*al-ṭuhūru shaṭr al-īmān*—cleanliness is a portion [or dimension] of the faith'.[18] This statement of the Prophet ﷺ truly permeates almost every aspect of Islam. The Qur'ān and *ḥadīth* are replete with detailed instruction on the cleanliness (*ṭahārah*) of body and attire in the context of ritual performances, the consumption of victuals, meat and drink, the cleanliness of one's living quarters, public places and thoroughfares, and moral and spiritual purity in general. Nearly every major work on *fiqh* and on Islam as a whole, as well as the major collections of *ḥadīth*, contain detailed chapters on the subject of *ṭahārah*, so that it becomes clear that purity is an integral part of the religion and an important attribute of Islamic personality, indeed of the personal dignity of the individual itself.

Dignity is also a right of the dead, which means that the body of deceased person must be treated with respect. It is forbidden to damage or break the bones of a dead person even if the effect of this may not be obvious. The Prophet thus declared in a *ḥadīth* that 'breaking a bone of the dead is like breaking one while he is alive'.[19]

كسر عظم الميت ككسره حيا.

An exception to this is when it may be necessary for medical purposes.[20] The jurists have differed on the permissibility of cutting open the womb of a deceased woman in order to save a foetus. This is not permissible, according to one view, as it violates the dignity and physical integrity of the deceased, and also the likelihood of saving the life of the foetus in such situations is not expected to be high. The Shāfiʿīs, Ḥanafīs and Mālikīs, however, have held that this is permissible if it could save the life of the foetus. The final decision must, to some extent, depend on the state of the art in medicine, and the accuracy of the expected results. Al-

Zuḥaylī has considered the permissive position preferable, not just for the purpose of saving the life of the foetus but also in other situations of necessity, such as in murder investigation where the cause of justice might depend on such internal examination. Organ transplantation, such as that of the eye or heart, is also permissible with the approval of an expert physician who is upright and reliable. This is because the interest of the living generally takes priority over that of the dead. To give eyesight to a person or help him or her live or overcome severe illness is an act of great merit and highly desirable from the perspective of *Sharīᶜah*.[21] It is, moreover, in due regard for the inherent dignity of man that selling human body parts, including the hair, skin and milk, is not lawful, although they may be donated as charity.[22] The basic principle regarding this is stated in the following *ḥadīth*: 'Everything that belongs to a Muslim is prohibited to his fellow Muslim: his blood, his property and his honour.'[23]

كل المسلم على المسلم حرام دمه وماله وعرضه.

The purport of this *ḥadīth* also applies to the dead insofar as the dead and the living are equal in regard to personal honour. This is also upheld in a legal maxim of *fiqh* which declares: 'The dignity of a deceased person is the same as if he or she were alive.'[24]

حرمة الانسان ميتاً كحرمته حيا.

Muslim jurists are unanimous that backbiting against the dead is forbidden, as is digging his or her grave or interfering with his or her remains.

Insulting a deceased person similarly falls under the same prohibitive rules that apply to the living. The Prophet ﷺ has strongly recommended that the dead should be remembered only for their virtues and not for their failings. Two reasons are given in the following *ḥadīth* for this, one of which is that the dead are unable to defend themselves against abuse, and the other is that insulting the dead hurts the feelings of their living relatives:

> Mention only the virtues of your deceased ones and avoid talking about their misdeeds.[25]

اذكروا محاسن موتاكم وكفوا عن مساويهم.

Avoid reviling the dead so that you do not hurt the feelings of their living relatives.[26]

لا تسبوا الأموات فتؤذوا به الأحياء.

To relate all this to the dignified character of the believer, the Prophet ﷺ declared in a *ḥadith*: 'The believer is not abusive, nor is he a slanderer, nor does he curse.'[27]

ليس المؤمن بالساب ولا بالطعان وباللعان.

The Prophet ﷺ also said the same about himself when he declared, 'I have not been sent to curse the people. I have been sent only as a mercy.'[28]

إني لم أبعث لعانا، إنما بعثت رحمة.

The physical manifestations of dignity in Islam are thus evident in the safeguards it provides against physical abuse, and in the care that the individual himself must take to ensure a dignified lifestyle. The *Sharīʿah* encourages the individual to take an uncompromising stand on matters of safety and health, and cautions him against irrational dogmatism, and against indulgence in risk-taking that jeopardises his self-image and equilibrium and causes him to be undignified.

NOTES

1. Muslim, *Mukhtaṣar Ṣaḥīḥ Muslim*, p. 484, *ḥadīth* no. 1833.
2. Reported by al-Ṭabarānī and quoted by Muḥammad al-Ghazālī, *Ḥuqūq al-Insān*, p. 55.
3. Al-Nawawī, *Riyāḍ al-Ṣāliḥīn*, *ḥadīth* no. 1667.
4. Muslim, *Mukhtaṣar Ṣaḥīḥ Muslim*, p. 186, *ḥadīth* no. 48
5. Al-Bukhārī, *Ṣaḥīḥ al-Bukhārī*, I, 110, *ḥadīth* no. 84.
6. Al-Tirmidhī, *Sunan al-Tirmidhī*, III, 255, *ḥadīth* no. 84.

7. Yaʿqūb ibn Ibrāhīm Abū Yūsuf, *Kitāb al-Kharāj*, 5th edn, Cairo, al-Maṭbaʿah al-Salafiyyah, 1396 AH, p. 164.

8. Ibn Taymiyyah *al-Siyāsah al-Sharʿiyyah*, p. 113.

9. Muslim, *Mukhtaṣar Ṣaḥīḥ Muslim*, p. 294, *ḥadīth* no. 1112.

10. Al-Tirmidhī, *Sunan al-Tirmidhī*, *ḥadīth* no. 147.

11. Muslim, *Mukhtaṣar Ṣaḥīḥ Muslim*, p. 474, *ḥadīth* no. 1784.

12. Mutajallī, *al-Ḥurriyyāt wa'l-Ḥuqūq*, p. 29.

13. Abū Zahrah, *Tanẓīm*, p. 28.

14. ʿAwdah, *al-Tashrīʿ al-Jinā'ī*, I, 448; ʿAdī Zayd Kaylānī, *Mafāhim al-Ḥaqq wa'l-Ḥurriyyah fi'l-Islām wa'l-Fiqh al-Waḍʿī*, Amman, Dār Bashīr li'l-Nashr wa'l-Tawzīʿ, 1410/1990, p. 169.

15. Ibn Mājah, *Sunan Ibn Mājah*, vol. II, p. 1395, *ḥadīth* no. 4168.

16. Al-Suyūtī, *al-Jāmiʿ al-Ṣaghir*, *ḥadīth* no. 3271.

17. Muslim, *Mukhtaṣar Ṣaḥīḥ Muslim*, p. 390, *ḥadīth* no. 1485.

18. Ibid., p. 41, *ḥadīth* no. 120

19. Al-Tabrīzī, *Mishkāt*, vol. I, *ḥadīth* no. 1714.

20. Yūsuf al-Qaraḍāwī, *al-Khaṣā'iṣ al-ʿĀmmah li'l-Islām*, Cairo, Maktabah Wahbah, 1409/1989, p. 79.

21. Cf. Zuḥaylī, *al-Fiqh al-Islāmī*, III, pp. 521-522.

22. Abū Zahrah, *Tanẓīm*, p. 30; Ibn ʿĀbidīn, *Ḥāshiyah*, IV, 139.

23. Al-Nawawī, *Riyāḍ al-Ṣāliḥīn*, *ḥadīth* no. 1535.

24. Al-Sibāʿī, *Ishtirākiyyāt al-Islām*, p. 71.

25. Al-Tabrīzī, *Mishkāt*, vol. I, *ḥadīth* no. 1678.

26. Ibid., vol. I, *ḥadīth* no. 4847.

27. Ibid., vol. III, *ḥadīth* no. 1822.

28. Muslim, *Mukhtaṣar Ṣaḥīḥ Muslim*, *Kitāb al-Birr wa'l-Ṣilla, Bāb Karāhiyāt al-Laʿnah*, *ḥadīth* no. 1822.

CHAPTER SIXTEEN

Dignity and the Objectives (*Maqāṣid*) of the *Sharīᶜah*

The five essential values of the *Sharīᶜah* on which the *ᶜulamā'* are in agreement, namely, faith, life, intellect, property and lineage, are all premised on the dignity of the human person, which must be protected as a matter of priority. These are the overriding objectives (*maqāṣid*) of the *Sharīᶜah* in that the entire range of the laws of *Sharīᶜah* are in one way or another intended to safeguard and promote these values. Although they combine the interests both of the individual and the community, the focus of these values is nevertheless on the individual. A firm commitment to protect these values is tantamount to the protection of human dignity.

The Mālikī jurist Shihāb al-Dīn al-Qarāfī added *al-ᶜirḍ*, that is, personal honour, to what the jurists have identified as the five essential values (i.e. *al-ḍaruriyyāt al-khamsah*) of the *Sharīᶜah.*[1] In adding *al-ᶜirḍ* to the existing list of five essential values, al-Qarāfī was aware that much of what would be relevant to *ᶜirḍ* would fall into the category of protecting lineage (*al-nasl*, *al-nasab*), but he apparently thought that this was not enough, which is why he added *al-ᶜirḍ* to the list. It will be noted in this connection that the origin of this five-fold identification of the essential goals of the *Sharīᶜah* is taken from the *ḥudud* (prescribed) punishments in the Qur'ān. These are deemed to signify a structure of values that the Qur'ān has protected under the pain of fixed penalties for such crimes as theft, adultery and slander. Al-Qarāfī has noted, however, that the Qur'ān makes slanderous accusation (*qadhf*) a separate *ḥadd* offence, that is, in addition to adultery (*zinā*), hence his addition of *al-ʿirḍ* as a separate value-point.[2]

Without wishing to enter into details, it may be added briefly that Ibn Taymiyyah criticised this whole approach of confining the scope of the basic values of the *Sharīʿah* to any specific number or themes. Ibn Taymiyyah held that the goals of the *Sharīʿah* (*maqāṣid al-Sharīʿah*) are numerous since they change with circumstance. He added, for example, freedom as a basic goal of the *Sharīʿah*, and maintained the view that the *maqāṣid* should be seen as an open chapter rather than a close circuit, as it were, leaving open the possibility of identifying new and additional values and goods. The contemporary scholar Yūsuf al-Qaraḍāwī is in agreement with Ibn Taymiyyah on this point, and has himself suggested that the welfare state should be recognised as one of the *maqāṣid* of the *Sharīʿah*. The present writer too recently wrote in an article that under present circumstances, research and development in science and technology merit recognition as some of the *maqāṣid* of the *Sharīʿah*.[3]

The *maqāṣid al-Sharīʿah* find their origin in the Qur'ān and *Sunnah*. No specific number or list of such objectives is found in these sources, but they do contain numerous references to such themes as the protection of life, honour, family and property, etc., which enabled the jurists to identify the five values referred to above as well as a number of other values that constitute the basic goals and objectives of the *Sharīʿah*, and are protected by its detailed rules.

Muslim jurists have divided the goals of *Sharīʿah* into the three categories of essential (*ḍarūriyyāt*), complementary (*ḥājiyyāt*) and embellishments (*taḥsīniyyāt*). The essential goals, or the five above-mentioned values, are so identified because of their foundational importance to the preservation of normal order in society and the survival and well being of individuals. The *Sharīʿah* takes detailed measure to protect these values. *Jihād* is thus validated to protect the faith, and so is the law of just retaliation (*qiṣāṣ*) to protect life. Theft, adultery and slanderous accusation are offences for which the *Sharīʿah* prescribes specified penalties (i.e. the *ḥudūd*) so as to protect personal property, family and the personal honour of the individual.[4]

The complementary objectives (*ḥājiyyāt*) seek to bring about comfort and repel severity and hardship. The *Sharīʿah* thus grants a series of concessions, in relation to obligatory duties, to the sick and disabled, pregnant women and travellers, which partake of the complementary objectives. The *Sharīʿah* also validates a number of contracts and transactions that are marked by some defect or imperfection, but because they fulfil a certain need and people have found them to be convenient to practice, the defect in them is ignored and they are validated as a result. There are contracts and transactions, for example, that are not free of *ribā'* (usury) and *gharar* (uncertainty and risk-taking) and others which fail to meet a certain requirement of the law of contract, which have been validated, either by the *Sunnah* or by consensus (*ijmā*ᶜ) of the jurists in order to facilitate trade and transactions between people, and meet their convenience.

The third category of the *maqāṣid*, namely the *taḥsīniyyāt*, seek to attain refinement and perfection in the personal lives of individuals and their interaction in society. The *Sharī*ᶜ*ah* thus encourages cleanliness beyond the minimum level that is required for the performance of certain rituals of worship; it also encourages beauty, leniency and compassion and promotes pleasant manners (*ḥusn al-khulq*) and fair dealing (*iḥsān*) among people, all of which partake of the *taḥsīniyyāt*.

Notwithstanding its obvious significance as a legal theory that promised versatility and dynamism, the *maqāṣid al-Sharī*ᶜ*ah* did not receive much attention in the early stages of the development of Islamic legal thought. The jurists of the first three centuries were preoccupied with *uṣūl al-fiqh*, or the science of the sources of law, and paid little attention to the *maqāṣid*. Even to this day, many a reputable textbook on *uṣūl al-fiqh* does not include *maqāṣid al-Sharī*ᶜ*ah* in of their coverage. This is due partly to the fact that the *maqāṣid* as a theme is largely concerned with the philosophy of the law, its outlook and objectives, and as such, did not blend well with the textualist doctrines and approaches of *uṣūl al-fiqh*. Since the Qur'ān and *Sunnah* consisted of the words of God and His Messenger, they are divine and the words themselves, rather than their goal and purposes, are the carriers of the *Sharī*ᶜ*ah*. The ᶜ*ulamā'* thus adopted a textualist approach to the formulation of *uṣūl al-fiqh* and shunned indulgence in theorisation about the goals and purposes of the law.

Imam al-Ḥaramayn al-Juwaynī (d. 478/1085) was probably the first to classify the *maqāṣid* into the three categories of essential, complementary and desirable, and these have gained general acceptance ever since. His student, Abū Ḥāmid al-Ghazālī (d. 505/1111), developed al-Juwaynī's ideas further, and identified the five interests noted above as the embodiment of the essential *maqāṣid*. A number of jurists continued to contribute to theories of the *maqāṣid*, but it was Abū Isḥāq Ibrāhīm al-Shāṭibī (d. 790/1388) who developed the *maqāṣid* into a prominent theme and chapter of the *Sharī*ᶜ*ah*, and devoted almost the entire length of the second of his four-volumed work, *al-Muwāfaqāt*, to the study of the *maqāṣid*.

As for the identification of the *maqāṣid*, some *ᶜulamā* have held that they are identified by reference to the textual injunctions (*nuṣūṣ*) of the *Sharīᶜah*, especially the commands and prohibitions. These are, in other words, the carriers of the *maqāṣid* and the latter have no separate existence outside this framework. This too was basically a textualist reading of the *maqāṣid*, which was upheld by the Ẓāhiriyyah, but the majority held that the *maqāṣid* might also be identified by reference to the cause (*ᶜillah*), and rationale (*ḥikmah*) of textual injunctions. The chief exponent of the *maqāṣid*, al-Shāṭibī, opened the scope of the *maqāṣid* further by saying that the *maqāṣid* may also be identified through a general and comprehensive reading of the text. This was what he called induction (*al-istiqrā'*). Al-Shāṭibī thus posed the following question: we know that the *maqāṣid* are known from the clear injunctions, but can they also be known from a general reading of the text, or even when the text has remained silent in respect of a certain value? To this, al-Shāṭibī gave an affirmative response through his proposed method of induction as explained below.

There may be various textual references to a subject, none of which may be in the nature of a decisive text, yet their collective weight is such that leaves no doubt as to the meaning that is conveyed by them. A decisive conclusion may, in other words, be arrived at from a plurality of speculative expressions. Al-Shāṭibī illustrated this by saying that nowhere in the Qur'ān is there a specific declaration to the effect that the *Sharīᶜah* has been enacted for the benefit of the people. Yet this is a definitive conclusion derived from the collective reading of a variety of textual proclamations.[5] Similarly, the validity of an act of worship (*ᶜibādah*) cannot be established by means of reasoning (*ijtihād*) in the absence of a particular text. This is also an inductive conclusion, which is drawn from the detailed evidence that exists on the subject. It is the same inductive method, which led the *ᶜulamā'* to the conclusion that protection of the five values (referred to above) is of primary importance to the *Sharīᶜah*, there being no textual ruling to specify any category of values in that order. Al-Shāṭibī added that the goals and benefits of the *Sharīᶜah* are to be understood in their broad and comprehensive sense, which include all benefits pertaining to this world and the next, those of the individual and the community, material, moral and spiritual benefits and those which relate to present as well as future generations.[6] Al-Shāṭibī also emphasised the importance of the *maqāṣid* to *ijtihād* and advised the jurist and *mujtahid* to pay special attention to the *maqāṣid*.

Since the *maqāṣid* are basically concerned with values that take human welfare as their focus, and they are unencumbered by the technicalities of the sort that fill the manuals of *uṣūl al-fiqh* on such themes as *ijmāᶜ*, *qiyās* and *istiḥsān* etc., they can be used more effectively to promote human dignity, human rights and welfare. As an instrument and theory of the *Sharīᶜah*, the *maqāṣid* can also be used to address issues of contemporary concern to the Muslims side by side perhaps with the much valued but somewhat technical and over burdened heritage of the science of *uṣūl al-fiqh*.

NOTES

1. The other two are known as *ḥājiyyāt* (complementary interests) and *taḥsīniyyāt* (embellishments).
2. Yūsuf al-Qarāḍawī, *Madkhal li-Dirāsah al-Sharīᶜah al-Islāmiyyah*, Cairo, Maktabah Wahbah, 1411/1991, p. 73.
3. Mohammad H. Kamali, 'Maqāṣid al-Sharīᶜah: The Objectives of Islamic Law', *Association of Muslim Lawyers Newsletter* (London), vol. 3, 1998, p. 14.
4. See for details see Mohammad H. Kamali, 'Maqāṣid al-Sharīᶜah: the Objectives of Islamic Law', *Islamic Studies* 3 (1999), pp. 193-209.
5. Abū Isḥāq Ibrāhīm al-Shāṭibī, *Muwāfaqāt fī Uṣūl al-Sharīᶜah*, ed. I. Ramaḍān, Beirut, Dār al-Maᶜrifah, 1994, II, 6; see also al-Qaraḍāwī, *Madkhal*, p. 58.
6. Al-Shāṭibī, *Muwāfaqāt*, I, 242.

CHAPTER SEVENTEEN

Dignity and the Issue of Basic Human Needs

Dignity can hardly become a reality when there is crushing poverty and degradation. The invalid, those who are poor and the sick can easily be led to despair in a society where compassion and selfless giving are regarded as insignificant. Moral teaching and religious advice are not always enough to ensure the assistance of the poor and the needy. To create the basis for a commitment to fulfil these needs, society needs the assurance of enforceable rules for equitable distribution of wealth. The existence, in other words, of effective measures by which the poor and the needy can claim financial support is necessary.

The Qur'ān speaks unequivocally of the basic right of the poor to a portion of the wealth of the affluent: 'In their wealth, there is a specified right for the needy and the deprived.' (al-Maʿārij, 70:24-25)

والذين في أموالهم حق معلوم للسائل والمحروم.

The *Sharīʿah* also imposes the *zakāh* tax, the maintenance of close relatives (*nafaqāt*), self-imposed penalties or expiations (*kaffārāt*), and other charities, 'so that wealth does not circulate among the rich alone' (al-Ḥashr, 59:7).

كي لا يكون دولة بين الأغنياء منكم.

The following *ḥadīth* may also be quoted in support of the basic commitment of the Islamic polity to the needy and the poor. The Prophet ﷺ thus declared in his capacity as the head of state:

> He who leaves behind property, it shall belong to his heirs, but if he leaves a debt or dependents in need, they shall be my responsibility.[1]

من ترك مالا فلورثته ومن ترك دينا أو ضياعا فليأتنى فأنا مولاه.

> The ruler is the supporter of he who has no supporter.[2]

السلطان ولي لمن لا ولي له.

> If one who has been made ruler over the affairs of Muslims does not strive for them, he will not enter the Garden with them. [3]

ما من أمير يلي أمر المسلمين ثم لا يجتهد لهم إلا لم يدخل الجنة معهم.

In another *ḥadīth* it is stated, clearly with reference to the leader, that 'one who does not exert himself in the affairs of Muslims is not one of them'.[4]

من لم يهتم بأمر المسلمين فليس منهم.

God Most High also promises distinction to those who 'for the love of God, feed the indigent, the orphan and the captive' (al-Insān, 76:8).

ويطعمون الطعام على حبه مسكيناً ويتيماً وأسيرا.

The Qur'ānic ruling on *zakāh* (legal alms) makes it at once a pillar of the faith and an obligation on those who possess assets above the exempted minimum for basic personal needs. *Zakāh* is payable at the annual rate of about two and a half per cent; it is a special tax earmarked for distribution among certain targeted groups, namely, the poor and the needy, insolvent debtors and a number of other classes of people (eight classes are mentioned in the Qur'ān, al-Tawbah, 9:60).

The issue of redistribution, or distributive justice, is a larger issue that cannot be adequately addressed here. Suffice it to say that it is due mainly to the strong and affirmative tone of the source evidence of the *Sharīᶜah* that the *ᶜulamā'* have spoken of the right of the poor and the needy to a decent standard of living in an Islamic state. Many have held this to include sufficient provisions in regard to food, shelter and clothing as well as medical treatment and, wherever necessary, domestic help. Modern writers on the subject have spoken of *al-takāful al-ijtimāᶜī* (social support), or the social security system, to which the Islamic state and society are committed and must strive to achieve.[5] Muslim jurists have also included among the social support measures of the *Sharīᶜah* such other varieties of assistance as helping the individual to get married, basic transportation allowances and the continuity of all this for at least one calendar year.[6]

The social support, or *takāful*, that Islam envisages is not just a question of financial assistance but also of fair and dignified treatment. Respect for elders, especially for one's parents, is a requirement of the faith. The Qur'ān thus stipulates, with regard to the rights of one's parents:

> Your Lord has decreed that you worship none but Him and that you be kind to your parents. Whether one or both of them attain old age in thy life, say not to them a word of contempt, nor repel them, but address them in dignified terms. And out of kindness, lower to them the wing of humility, and say 'My Lord! Bestow on them Your mercy as they cherished me in childhood. (al-Isrā', 17:23-24)

وقضى ربك ألا تعبدوا إلا إياه وبالوالدين إحساناً إما يبلغنّ عندك
الكبر أحدهما أو كلا هما فلا تقل لهما أف ولا تنهر هما وقل
لهما قولاً كريما واخفض لهما جناح الذل من الرحمة وقل رب
ارحمهما كما ربياني صغيرا.

It is indicative of special emphasis that the duty of respect for parents appears in this text next to the worship of God. Indeed it is not just respect but cherishing kindness and humility to parents that is recommended. The juxtaposition of worshipping God and honouring one's parents also signifies that parental love should be to the Muslims a type of divine love: nothing that we can do can ever really compensate for what we have received from our parents or from God. The spiritual significance of this injunction may also be that we cannot expect God's forgiveness if we are rude and unkind to those who unselfishly brought us up. In another place, God proclaims that, 'We have enjoined upon mankind kindness to the parents' (al-Aḥqāf, 46:15, see also al-Nisā', 4:36).

ووصينا الإنسان بوالديه إحسانا.

Abū Ḥurayrah reported that a man asked the Messenger of God and said to him: 'O Messenger of God! Who has the greatest claim to my best treatment?' The Prophet ﷺ said 'Your mother.' Then the man asked, 'And then who?' The Prophet ﷺ said, 'Your mother.' He asked again, 'And then who?' The Prophet ﷺ said, 'Your mother.' He asked again, 'And who then?' to which the Prophet ﷺ replied, 'Your father.'[7]

يا رسول اللّه من أحق الناس بحسن صحابتي؟ قال: أمك، قال: ثم من؟ قال: أمك، قال ثم من؟ قال: أمك، قال: ثم من؟ قال: أبوك.

The rules of Islamic law that entitle close relatives to maintenance (*nafaqah*) usually require that the relative in question is in need of support and is unable to earn a living. Parents are an exception to the rule of need because of the Qur'ānic call that they should be treated with kindness at all times.

The view is now prevalent among Muslim scholars that *zakāh,* which is in any case an entitlement of the very poor, the obligatory maintenance of close relatives (*niẓām al-nafaqāt*) and inheritance (*mīrāth*) are not enough to ensure the objectives of distributive justice in contemporary Muslim societies.[8] In response to this, many have cited the view taken by earlier jurists, including Imām Mālik, Ibn Ḥazm al-Ẓāhirī and al-Qurṭubī, to the effect that the state may impose additional taxes on the rich if *zakāh* revenues are insufficient to meet the needs of the poor.[9] The rich are also encouraged to give extra money to the poor, in addition to the *zakāh* they pay, as and when they see the need for this. There is no specific *quorum* or limit on this, but it should be given in accordance with one's ability. The poor among one's relatives have a greater entitlement to generosity and compassion than people at large. Thus according to a *ḥadīth*, 'Charity to the poor is charity, and charity to a relative is in two kinds: charity and affection, that is, goodness and compassion'.[10]

الصدقة على المسكين صدقة، وعلى ذوى الرحم ثنتان، صدقة وصلة، أى بر وعطف.

This is endorsed in yet another *ḥadīth* where the Prophet ﷺ is reported to have said: 'One who wishes his wealth to increase, and his life to be blessed [with God's benevolence] let him take good care of the ties of kinship.'[11]

من أحب أن يبسط له في رزقه وينسأ له في أثره فليصل رحمه.

The Prophet ﷺ added emphasis to this when he addressed his community in the following terms: 'O *ummah* of Muḥammad! By the One who sent me with the truth, He will not accept charity that a man gives to others while his own relatives are in need of his support. By the One in whose hand my life reposes, He will not look at such a man on the Day of Judgement.'[12]

يا أمة محمد والذي بعثني بالحق لا يقبل صدقة من رجل وله قرابة يحتاجون الى صلته ويصرفها إلى غيرهم، والذى نفسي بيده لا ينظر اللّه إليه يوم القيامة.

A more recent contributor to this theme is Bāqir al-Ṣadr, who has made a case, in his renowned work *Iqtiṣāadunā* (Our Economy), for a minimum guaranteed standard of living for all in an Islamic state. ʿUmar Chapra and Nejatullah Siddiqi have also spoken in support of al-Ṣadr's views.

According to the classical Islamic model, there is to be no distinction, in the entitlement to financial support, between Muslim and non-Muslim citizens. The welfare responsibility of the state toward citizens extends to all alike. Saʿīd ibn al-Musayyib has reported that the Prophet ﷺ used to give charity to a Jewish family, and the allocation that they received was continued after the Prophet's demise.

The wife of the Prophet ﷺ, Ṣafiyyah, also gave charity to some of her relatives who were Jewish.[13] There is also evidence that the second Caliph, ʿUmar ibn al-Khaṭṭāb, entitled the Jews to welfare assistance, especially in view of the fact that non-Muslim citizens at that time were liable to the payment of poll-tax (*jizyah*).[14] There were also cases in which the Caliph ʿUmar exempted some poor non-Muslims from the payment of *jizyah* and assigned for them an allowance from the public treasury. He is reported, in this connection, to have cited the Qur'ānic *āyah* which provides that 'charities are only for the poor (*al-fuqarā'*) and the needy (*al-masākīn*)' (al-Tawba, 9:60) and said that *al-fuqarā'* referred to the poor among Muslims, and *al-masākīn* to the poor among non-Muslims.[15] This is no longer imposed on non-Muslim citizens today simply because the tax laws that are currently in force in Muslim countries make no distinction between Muslims and non-Muslims and apply a regime of uniform taxation. There remains no basis therefore for a separate tax to be imposed on non-Muslims. Al-Qaraḍāwī has suggested, and rightly so, that both Muslims and non-Muslims may pay the *zakāh* tax in order to assist the poor. To pay the *zakāh* is a religious duty for Muslims but there is no objection if non-Muslims also volunteer to pay it as a substitute to what would have been a poll-tax in earlier times.[16] The fact that non-Muslim citizens are expected to contribute to military service has led another observer to write that 'this should automatically mean their exemption from *jizyah*'.[17]

NOTES

1. Al-Bukhārī, *Ṣaḥīḥ al-Bukhārī*, II, 155.
2. Abū Dāwūd, *Sunan*, I, 148.
3. Ibid., *ḥadīth* no. 2948.
4. Abū ʿAdb Allāh al-Ḥākim, *al-Mustadrak ʿalā al-Ṣaḥīḥayn*, Aleppo (Syria), Maktab al-Maṭbuʿāt al-Islamiyyah, n.d., IV, 320; al-Sibāʿī, *Ishtirākiyyat*, p. 149; al-ʿĪlī, *Ḥurriyyāt*, p. 496.
5. Abū Zahrah, *Tanẓīm*, p. 152; al-Qaraḍāwī, *Khaṣā'iṣ*, p. 79
6. Al-Qaraḍāwī, *Khaṣā'iṣ*, p. 80.
7. Al-Mundhirī, *al-Targhīb wa'l-Tarhīb*, IV, 100.
8. For a summary on this view see Rodney Wilson's article on Baqir al-Sadr's 'Contribution to Islamic Economics' in *Journal of Islamic Studies*, vol. 9, no. 1 (January 1998), p. 53.

9. Abū ʿAlī Ibn Ḥazm, *al-Muḥallā*, ed. Aḥmad M. Shākir, 7 vols., Cairo, Dār al-Fikr, n.d., III, 56.

10. Al-Mundhirī, *al-Targhīb wa'l-Tarhīb*, II, 160.

11. Al-Nawawī, *Riyāḍ al-Ṣālihin*, *ḥadīth* no. 324.

12. Al-Mundhirī, *al-Targhīb wa'l-Tarhīb*, II, 161; al-Badawī, *Daʿā'im*, p. 524.

13. Al-Qāsim ibn Salām Abū ʿUbayd, *Kitāb al-Amwāl*, ed. Muḥammad Ḥāmid al-Faqī, Riyāḍ, Maṭbaʿah ʿAbd al-Laṭīf Ḥijāzī, 1353 AH, p. 84; al-Badawī, *Daʿā'im*, p. 524.

14. Abū Yūsuf, *al-Kharāj*, p. 126; Ghanoushi, *Ḥuqūq al-Muwāṭanah*, p. 90.

15. Abū Yūsuf, *al-Kharāj*, p. 150; al-Badawī, *Daʿā'im*, p. 525.

16. Yūsuf al-Qaraḍāwī, *Fiqh al-Zakāh*, 3rd edn., Beirut, Mu'assasat al-Risālah, 1397/1977, vol. 1, pp. 98-99.

17. Tawfīq al-Shāwī, in his Preface to Ghanouchi, *Ḥuqūq al-Muwāṭanah*, p. 27.

Conclusion

It may be said in conclusion that the commitment of the *Sharīʿah* to the dignity of man is so strong and pervasive as to warrant the identification of human dignity as one of the higher goals and objectives (*maqāṣid*) of the *Sharīʿah*. This means that the dignity of man is identified as a strategic value of overall significance, and therefore all measures that are devised to protect and promote human dignity are *a priori* upheld and sanctified by the *Sharīʿah*. An explicit commitment of this kind in the applied constitutions of present-day Muslim countries is highly recommended, if only to show a visible commitment to the clear mandates of the Qur'ān. It is arguable, therefore, that the constitutions of Muslim countries should take human dignity as a postulate and framework that is then taken to its logical conclusion in the detailed formulations of the basic rights and liberties that are upheld and guaranteed therein.

Islam's perception of human dignity is predicated on the unity in origin of mankind, and its basic equality in regard to the essence of humanity, rights and obligations. Islam's outlook on moral values, and the basic ethical norms that constitute the foundation of affirmative social and human relations, is also essentially monolithic. Human dignity, human rights and human obligations gain strength and substance when they are accepted and supported by mankind as a whole. For these are shared values and aspirations and must therefore be founded on commitment to a shared agenda and framework. Kofi Annan has voiced this sentiment when he observed that 'there is not one law for one continent and one for another. And there should be only one single standard—a universal standard—for judging human rights violations'.[1] The alternative is lip-service to values that can only be expected to be skin-deep, especially in societies where general equality and other basic rights are talked about but are in reality not recognised, or only partially recognised. Commitment to the same, ethical standards ensures commoness of purpose, and adds meaning to what may otherwise amount to little more than rhetoric. A shared and genuine commitment is necessary in order to wage a successful campaign against prejudice, poverty and degradation.

Cultural diversity and differences of method need not be seen as compromising this essential unity of values. These diversities have always existed and they exist even among communities within the same country or cultural zone. Even before one nurtures the ideal of essential harmony in regard to human dignity, it is necessary to widen one's horizons to accept differences at various levels. The purpose of this is to develop unity on essential ethical norms and basic human rights while recognising, in the meantime, differences of culture, custom and religion. For diversity within unity is a familiar description that has often been given to Islam itself, and its *Sharīᶜah*, a characterisation that can also be said to be true of Western legal and cultural traditions. The wide basis of support for the Universal Declaration of Human Rights in the Muslim world remains undiminished. The former chairman of the UN Commission on Human Rights, and current leader of the Malaysian Delegation to that Commission, Musa Hitam, voiced this sentiment when he said that, 'The Declaration should be universally accepted as a code of conduct for the use of states and individuals. Indeed the Declaration contains the teachings of all the major religions of the world and merits adherence as close as possibile by all.' *The Star*, a daily broadsheet of Kuala Kumpur, which carried Musa Hitam's interview, published, in commemoration of the 50th anniversary of the UDHR, the text of the entire Declaration.[2]

The awareness that the Universal Declaration of Human Rights exhibits a certain degree of Western bias, at the level of culture rather than basic values perhaps, and should therefore seek to integrate other cultural postulates, has not meant and should not mean its rejection or derogation by the Muslim world or countries that subscribe to different cultural traditions. The Prophet Muḥammad ﷺ has said that 'wisdom is the lost property of the believer' (*al-ḥikmatu ḍāllatu al-mu'min*) and also that 'religion is good advice (*al-dīnu al-naṣīḥatu*). It would thus go contrary to the advice of these sagacious statements either to act or speak disparagingly of the UDHR. But, as 'we mark the fiftieth anniversary of the Universal Declaration of Human Rights,' as Sinnar rightly observes, 'we should not refrain from the conceptual challenge of questioning the contemporary understanding of human rights—not to undermine it, but to enhance our universal quest for a more just and more humane world'.[3] Muslim countries have in fact spoken in support of the UDHR, and this is only right. But it is also right to try to enhance the universal appeal of this charter, and make it the product of shared aspirations and efforts by all concerned. Then one might hope to make the UDHR an integral part of the constitutions of the member states of the United Nations. This might well mark a new era for a more participatory and comprehensive UDHR, one that was more genuinely universal, and inspired commitment from within, that is, at the level of the national charter and constitution.

NOTES

1. *The Star*, 'Weighing Our Rights and Freedoms', 10 December 1998, Section 2, p. 3.
2. *The Star*, 10 December 1998, Section 2, pp. 3ff.
3. Sinnar, 'Reflection', p. 4.

Glossary

ʿAbd: servant.
ʿAdalah: uprightness of character; justice.
Amānah: trust (pl. *amānāt*).
Al-asmāʾ al-ḥusnā: the Most Beautiful Names of God.
Āyah (pl. *āyāt*)*:* a verse of the Qurʾān.
Awqāf (sing. *waqf*)*:* charitable endowments.
Bayʿah: pledge of allegiance given to a newly elected leader or Caliph.
Ḍarūrah: necessity.
Ḍarūriyāt al-khamsah: the five essential value of life, faith, property, intellect and lineage.
Daʿwah: call to the faith; invitation to embrace Islam.
Diyyah: blood money.
Faqīr (pl. *fuqarāʾ*)*:* poor.
Farḍ ʿayn: personal obligation of the individual, especially in respect of religious duties.
Farḍ kifāʾī: collective obligation of the community as a whole.
Fiqh: Islamic law as developed by Muslim jurists. The term is often used synonymously with *Sharīʿah.*
Fusūq: inequity; outrage.
Gharar: uncertainty; risk-taking (of transactions).
Ḥaḍānah: the right of custody over infants.
Ḥadīth: lit. speech; the reported sayings and teachings of the Prophet Muḥammad ﷺ.
Ḥajjat al-widāʿ: the Prophet Muḥammad's ﷺ farewell Pilgrimage.
Ḥalāl: legitimate; allowed by the *Sharīʿah.*
Ḥaqq ṭabīʿī: natural right/law.

Ḥarām: totally forbidden by the *Sharīʿah.*
Ḥayā': humility.
Ḥikmah: rationale (of law); wisdom.
Ḥisbah: promotion of good and prevention of evil.
Ḥudūd: (pl. of *ḥadd*)*:* textually prescribed punishment.
Ḥurriyyat al-muʿāraḍah: freedom to criticise government leaders.
Ḥusn al-khulq: good character.
Iḍāfī: inherently relative.
Iḥrām: seamless white garment worn during *ḥajj.*
Iḥsān: goodness; excellence; benevolence.
Ijmāʿ: consensus of opinion, especially of Muslim jurists over a ruling of the *Sharīʿah.*
Ijtihād: lit. 'exertion' and technically the effort a jurist makes in order to deduce the law which is not self-evident from its sources.
ʿIllah: cause.
Iltiqāṭ: saving and protecting an abandoned child.
ʿIrḍ: dignity.
Isti'nās: seeking permission.
Istiqrā': induction.
ʿIzzah: dignified status; honour.
Jihād: lit. struggle, in both the moral sense of struggling against evil or striving for excellence, and also in the physical sense of armed struggle for a holy cause.
Jizyah: the Islamic poll-tax.
Kabā'ir (sing. *kabīrah*)*:* major sins.
Kaffārah: expiation.
Khalīfah: Caliph; vicegerent; successor.
Khilāfah: lit. succession but commonly used to signify the vicegerency of man in the earth. It also refers to the historical caliphate.
Kufr: lit. concealing or covering; denial of Islam by one's words and conduct; disbelief; infidelity.
Laqīt: abandoned infant.
Mafsadah: matter of civil disorder.
Maqāṣid (pl. of *maqṣad*)*:* goals and objectives (usually with reference to the *Sharīʿah*).
Maʿrūf: recognised good.
Masākīn (sing. *miskīn*)*:* needy.
Maṣlaḥah: (pl. *maṣāliḥ*), public interest or benefit.
Mirā' (also *mumārāt*)*:* acrimony; pointless squabbling that mars the atmosphere of fraternity and good will.

Mīrāth: inheritance, heritage.
Muʿāmalah: civil or commercial transaction, often used in contradistinction to *ʿibādah* (devotional matter)
Mufti: judge.
Muḥtasib: the officer in charge of *ḥisbah.*
Mujtahid: a legist competent enough to formulate an independent opinion based on the traditional sources, in matters legal or theological.
Mutawallī: trustee.
Muwakkil: plaintiff.
Nafaqah: right to maintenance between close relatives.
Naṣīḥah: sincere advice often offered at the initiative of its donor.
Nasl (or *nasab*)*:* lineage
Nisbī: relative
Nuṣūṣ (pl. *naṣṣ*)*:* textual injunctions.
Qadhf: slanderous accusation.
Qādhif: the perpetrator of *qadhf*; slander.
Qāḍī: judge versed in the *Sharīʿah.*
Qiblah: direction of prayer.
Qiṣāṣ: just/legal retaliation.
Qiyās: legal analogy.
Rifq: gentleness.
Ṣalāh: ritual prayer.
Salām: peace; the Islamic greeting ' Peace be upon you', exchanged by Muslims whenever they meet.
Samāḥah: magnanimity, generosity, liberality.
Shūrā: consultation.
Ṣillah: kinship ties.
Taʿabbudī: devotional.
Ṭahārah: cleanliness of body and attire; ritual state of purity.
Tajassus: spying.
Takāful al-ijtimāʿī: social security system.
Takāful: social support.
Taklīf: liability; obligation.
Tanaṭṭuʿ: hair-splitting.
Taqwā: piety; God-consciousness.
Taʿrīf: informing; making known; notification; definition.
Taskhīr: subjugation of universe to man.
Taslīm: greeting.
Taʿzīr: lit. deterrence or deterrent punishment which a *qāḍī* may impose at his discretion by reference to attending circumstances.

Tawḥīd: belief in the Oneness of God; the doctrine of monotheism in Islam.
Ukhuwwah: fraternity.
ʿUlamāʾ (sing. *ʿālim*)*:* religious scholars; theologians.
Ulū al-amr: persons in charge of the community affairs.
Ummah: the worldwide Muslim community.
Uṣūl al-fiqh: sources of roots of Islamic law and jurisprudence; refers mainly to the Qur'ān and *Sunnah* as the principal sources of the *Sharīʿah*, but also to a number of other sources and methods which are used in order to facilitate the proper exercise of *ijtihād*.
Wakālah: agency; representation.
Wakīl: agent; representative.
Walī: guardian (usually of a minor person).
Waʿz: kindly admonition.
Zakāh: lit. 'purification', legal alms, a religious tax levied on the rich in order to help the poor.
Ẓann: suspicion.
Ẓann al-mubāḥ: permissible suspicion.
Ẓinā: adultery and fornication; extra-marital sexual intercourse.
Ẓulm: injustice.

Bibliography

Abū Dāwūd, *Sunan Abū Dāwūd*, Eng. trans. Aḥmad Ḥasan, 3 vols., Lahore: Ashraf Press, 1984.

Abū Ḥabīb, Saᶜdī, *Dirāsah fī Minhāj al-Islām al-Siyāsī*, Beirut: Mu'assasat al-Risālah, 1406/1985.

Abū ᶜUbayd, al-Qāsim b. Salām, *Kitāb al-Amwāl*, ed. Muḥammad Ḥāmid al-Faqī, Riyād: Maṭbaᶜat ᶜAbd al-Laṭīf Ḥijāzī, 1353 AH.

Abū Yūsuf, Yaᶜqūb b. Ibrāhīm, *Kitāb al-Kharāj*, 5th edn, Cairo: al-Maṭbaᶜah al-Salafiyyah, 1396 AH.

Abū Zahrah, Muḥammad, *al-Jarīmah wa'l-ᶜUqūbah fi'l-Fiqh al-Islāmī*, Cairo: Dār al-Fikr al-ᶜArabī, n.d.

——*al-Mujtamaᶜ al-Insānī fī Ẓill al-Islām*, 2nd edn, Jeddah: Dār al-Ṣuᶜūdiyyah, 1401/1981.

——*Tanẓīm al-Islām li'l-Mujtamaᶜ*, Cairo: Dār al-Fikr al-ᶜArabī, 1385/1965.

Al-Alūsi, Maḥmūd b. ᶜAbd Allāh, *Rūḥ al-Maᶜānī fī Tafsīr al-Qur'ān al-ᶜAẓīm*, Beirut: Dār al-Turāth al-ᶜArabī, n.d.

ᶜAmmārah, Muḥammad, *al-Islām wa Ḥuqūq al-Insān: Ḍarūrāt lā Ḥuqūq*, Cairo: Dār al-Shurūq, 1409/1989.

Al-ᶜAsqalānī, Aḥmad b. ᶜAlī b. Hajar, *Jawāhir Ṣaḥīḥ al-Bukhārī*, ed. ᶜIzz al-Dīn Sinwān, Beirut: Dār Iḥyā' al-ᶜUlūm, 1407/1987.

ᶜAwdah, ᶜAbd al-Qādir, *al-Tashrīᶜ al-Jinā'ī al-Islāmī*, Beirut: Mu'assasat al-Risālah, 1403/1983.

Al-Badawī, Ismāᶜīl. *Daᶜā'im al-Ḥukm fi'l-Sharīᶜah al-Islāmiyyah wa'l-Nuẓūm al-Dustūriyyah al-Muᶜāṣirah*, Cairo: Dār al-Fikr al-ᶜArabī, 1400/1980.

Al-Bahī, Muḥammad, *al-Dīn wa'l-Dawlah min Tawjīhāt al-Qur'ān al-Karīm*, Beirut: Dār al-Fikr, 1391/1971.

Al-Bukhārī, Muḥammad b. Ismāʿīl, *Ṣaḥīḥ al-Bukhārī*, Eng. trans. Muḥammad Muḥsin Khān, 6th edn, 9 vols., Lahore: Kazi Publications, 1986.

Cumaraswamy Param, 'The Universal Declaration of Human Rights—Is it Universal?', *Insaf: The Journal of the Malaysia Bar*, XXVI, no. 4 (December 1997).

Al-Dughmī, Muḥammad Rākān, *Al-Tajassus wa Aḥkāmuhu fī'l-Sharīʿah al-Islāmiyyah*, 2nd edn, Cairo: Dār al-Salām li'l-Ṭibāʿah wa'l-Nashr, 1406/1986.

—*Ḥimāyat al-Ḥayāt al-Khāṣṣah fi'l-Sharīʿah al-Islāmiyyah*, Cairo: Dār al-Salam li'l-Tibāʿah wa'l-Nashr, 1405/1985.

Ghanouchi, Rashīd, *Ḥuqūq al-Muwāṭanah: Ḥuqūq ghayr al-Muslim fi'l-Mujtamaʿ al-Islāmī*, 2nd edn, Herndon (VA): International Institute of Islamic Thought, 1413/1993.

Al-Ghazālī, Abū Ḥāmid Muḥammad, *Iḥyā' ʿUlūm al-Dīn*, 2nd edn, 5 vols., Cairo: Dār al-Fikr, 1400/1980.

Al-Ghazālī, Muḥammad, *Ḥuqūq al-Insān bayn Taʿālīm al-Islām wa Iʿlān al-Umam al-Muttaḥidah*, Alexandria (Egypt): Dār al-Daʿwah li'l-Nashr wa'l-Tawzīʿ, 1413/ 1993.

Al-Ḥākim, Abū ʿAbd Allāh al-Nishāpūrī, *Al-Mustadrak ʿalā al-Ṣaḥīḥayn,* Aleppo (Syria): Maktab al-Maṭbūʿāt al-Islāmiyyah, n.d.

Ibn ʿAbd Rabbih, Aḥmad al-Andalusī, *al-ʿIqd al-Farīd li'l-Malik al-Saʿīd*, 3rd edn, 15 vols., Cairo: Matbaʿah Lajnat al-Ta'līf 1384/1965.

Ibn ʿĀbidin, Muḥammad Amīn, *Ḥāshiyah Radd al-Mukhtār ʿalā Durr al-Mukhtār*, 2nd edn, Cairo: Muṣṭafā al-Bābī al-Ḥalabī, 1386/1966.

Ibn Ḥanbal, *Fihris Aḥādīth Musnad al-Imām Aḥmad Ibn Ḥanbal*, compiled by Abū Hājir Zaghlūl, Beirut: Dār al-Kutub, 1405/1985.

Ibn Ḥazm, Muḥammad ʿAlī b. Aḥmad, *al-Muḥallā*, ed. Aḥmad M. Shākir, 7 vols., Cairo: Dār al-Fikr, n.d.

Ibn Hishām, ʿAbd al-Mālik, *al-Sīrah al-Nabawiyyah*, 2 vols., Cairo Muṣṭafā al-Bābī al-Ḥalabī, 1936.

Ibn Kathīr, al-Ḥāfiz, *Tafsīr al-Qur'ān al-ʿAẓīm* (also known as *Tafsīr Ibn Kathīr*), 4 vols., Cairo: Dār al-Shaʿb, 1393/1973.

Ibn Mājah, Muḥammad b. Yazīd al-Qazwīnī, *Sunan Ibn Mājah*, 5 vols., Istanbul: Cagri Yayinlari, 1401/1981.

Ibn Qayyim, Al-Jawziyyah, *Iʿlām al-Muwaqqiʿīn ʿan Rabb al-ʿĀlamīn*, ed. Muḥammad Munīr al-Dimashqī, Cairo: Idārat al-Ṭibāʿah al-Munīriyyah, n.d.

——*Zād al-Maʿād fī Hudā Khayr al-ʿIbād,* Mecca: al-Maṭbaʿah al-Makkiyyah, n.d.

Ibn Taymiyyah, Tāqi al-Dīn, *al-Siyāsah al-Sharʿiyyah fī Iṣlāh al-Rāʿī wa'l-Rāʿiyyah,* 2nd edn, Cairo: Dār al-Kitāb al-ʿArabī, 1951.

Al-ʿĪlī, ʿAbd al-Ḥakīm Ḥasan, *al-Ḥurriyyāt al-ʿĀmmah,* Cairo: Dār al-Fikr, 1403/1983.

Al-Jundī, Ḥusni, *Ḍamānāt Ḥurmat al-Ḥayāt al-Khāṣṣah fi'l-Islām,* Cairo: Dār al-Naḥdah al-ʿArabiyyah, 1413/1993.

Kamali, Mohammad Hashim, 'Siyasah Sharʿiyyah or the Policies of Islamic Government', *The American Journal of Islamic Social Sciences,* 6 (1989), pp. 59-81.

——'The Limits of Power in an Islamic State', *Islamic Studies* 28 (1989), pp. 323-353.

——*Freedom of Expression in Islam,* 2nd edn, Cambridge: The Islamic Texts Society, 1997.

——'Maqāṣid al-Sharīʿah: The Objectives of Islamic Law', *Association of Muslim Lawyers Newsletter* (London), vol. 3, 1998, pp. 13-20.

——'Maqāṣid al-Sharīʿah: The Objectives of Islamic Law', *Islamic Studies* 3 (1999), pp. 193-209.

Kaylānī, ʿAdī Zayd, *Mafāhim al-Ḥaqq wa'l-Ḥurriyyah fi'l-Islām wa'l-Fiqh al-Waḍʿī,* Amman: Dār Bashīr li'l-Nashr wa'l-Tawzīʿ, 1410/1990.

Al-Khālidi, Maḥmud ʿAbd al-Majīd, *Maʿālim al-Khilāfah fi'l-Fikr al-Siyāsī al-Islāmī,* Beirut: Dār al-Jīl, 1404/1984.

Madkūr, Muḥammad Salām, *al-Fiqh al-Islāmi: al-Madkhal wa'l-Amwāl wa'l-Ḥuqūq wa'l-ʿUqūd,* 2nd edn, Cairo: Maṭbaʿat al-Fajalah, 1955.

Mahmassānī, Ṣubḥī, *Arkān Ḥuqūq al-Insān fi'l-Islām,* Beirut, Dār al-ʿIlm li'l-Malāyīn, 1979.

Al-Maqdisī, Shams al-Dīn ʿAbd Allāh b. Maflah al-Ḥanbalī, *al-Ādāb al-Sharʿiyyah wa'l-Minaḥ al-Marʿiyyah,* Cairo: Maṭbaʿat al-Manār, 1348 AH.

Al-Mubārakfūrī, Muḥammad ʿAbd al-Raḥmān, *Tuḥfat al-Ahwāzī bi-Sharḥ Jamiʿ al-Tirmidhī,* ed. ʿAbd al-Raḥmān ʿUthmān, 3rd edn, Beirut: Dār al-Fikr, 1399/1979.

Al-Mundhirī, Zakī al-Dīn ʿAbd al-ʿAẓīm, *al-Targhīb wa'l-Tarhīb,* 2 vols., Cairo: Musṭafā al-Bābī al-Ḥalabī, 1373/1954.

Mutajallī, Muḥammad Rajā', *al-Ḥurriyyāt wa'l-Ḥuqūq fi'l-Islām,* Rābitat al-ʿAlam al-Islāmī bi-Makkah al-Mukarramah: Dār al-Ṣaḥāfah wa'l-Nashr, 1407/1987.

Al-Nabhān, Muḥammad Fārūq, *Niẓām al-Ḥukm fi'l-Islām*. Kuwait: Jāmiᶜat al-Kuwait, 1974.

Al-Nawawī, Muḥyī al-Dīn. *Riyāḍ al-Ṣāliḥīn*, ed. Muḥammad Nāṣir al-Dīn al-Albānī, 2nd edn, Beirut: Dār al-Maktab al-Islāmī, 1404/1984.

Al-Nishāpūrī, Muslim b. Ḥajjāj, *Mukhtaṣar Ṣaḥīḥ Muslim*, ed. Muḥammad Nāṣir al-Dīn al-Albānī, 2 vols., Beirut: Dār al-Maktab al-Islāmī, 1404/1984.

Pannikar, Raimondo. 'Is the Notion of Human Rights a Western Concept?', *Interculture* (Montreal), vol. 17 no. 1 (March 1982), p. 28.

Al-Qādirī, ᶜAbd Allāh b. Aḥmad, *al-Kifā'ah al-Idāriyyah fi'l-Siyāsah al-Sharᶜiyyah*, Jeddah: Dār al-Mujtamaᶜ li'l-Nashr wa'l-Tawzīᶜ, 1406/1986.

Al-Qaraḍāwī, Yūsuf, *al-Khaṣā'iṣ al-ᶜĀmmah li'l-Islām*, Cairo: Maktabah Wahbah, 1409/1989.

——*Fiqh al-Zakāh*, 3rd edn, Beirut: Mu'assasat al-Risālah, 1397/1977.

——*Madkhal li-Dirāsah al-Sharīᶜah al-Islāmiyyah*. Cairo: Maktabah Wahbah, 1411/1991.

——*Min Fiqh al-Dawlah fi'l-Islām*, Cairo: Dār al-Shurūq, 1417/1997.

Quṭb, Sayyid, *al-ᶜAdālah al-Ijtimāᶜiyyah fi'l-Islām*, 4th edn, Cairo ᶜIsā al-Bābī al-Ḥalabī, 1373/1954.

Al-Sarakhsī, Shams al-Dīn Muḥammad, *al-Mabsūṭ*, 15 vols., Beirut, Dār al-Maᶜrifah, 1406/1986.

Al-Shāfiᶜī, Muḥammad b. Idrīs, *Kitāb al-Umm*, ed. Muḥammad Sayyid Kaylāni, 2nd edn, 6 vols., Cairo: Muṣṭafā al-Bābī al-Ḥalabī, 1403/1983.

Shaltūt, Maḥmūd, *al-Islām: ᶜAqīdah wa Sharīᶜah*, Kuwait: Maṭbaᶜ Dār al-Qalam, 1966.

Al-Shāṭibi, Abū Isḥāq Ibrāhīm, *Muwāfaqāt fī Uṣūl al-Sharīᶜah*, ed. I. Ramaḍān, 58 vols., Beirut: Dār al-Maᶜrifah, 1994.

Al-Sibāᶜī, Musṭafā, *Ishtirākiyyat al-Islām*, 2nd edn, Damascus al-Dār al-Qawmiyyah li'l-Ṭibāᶜah wa'l-Nashr, 1379/1960.

Sinnar, Shirin, 'Reflection on the 50th Anniversary of the Universal Declaration of Human Rights'. *Commentary: International Movement for a Just World* (Kuala Lumpur), new series, no. 19 (December 1998), pp. 1-5.

The Star, *Kuala Lumpur*.

Al-Suyūṭī, Jalāl al-Dīn, *al-Jāmiᶜ al-Ṣaghīr*, 4th edn, 2 vols, Cairo: Muṣṭafā al-Bābī al-Ḥalabī, 1954.

al-Ṭabarī, Muḥammad b. Jarīr, *Ta'rīkh al-Rusul wa'l-Mulūk*, Cairo: al-Maṭbaᶜah al-Tijāriyyah, 1358/1939.

Al-Tabrīzī, ᶜAbd Allāh al-Khaṭīb, *Mishkāt al-Maṣabīḥ*, ed. Muḥammad Nāṣir al-Dīn al-Albāni, 2nd edn, Beirut: al-Maktab al-Islāmī, 1399/1979.

Al-Tabrīzī, ᶜAbd Allāh al-Khaṭīb, *Mishkāt al-Maṣabīḥ*, Eng. trans. James Robson, Lahore: Ashraf Press, n.d.

Al-Tirmidhī, Abū ᶜĪsā Muḥammad, *Sunan al-Tirmidhī*, 3 vols., Beirut: Dār al-Fikr, 1400/1980.

Weeramantry, J. *Islamic Jurisprudence: An International Perspective*, Basingstoke (UK): Macmillan, 1988.

Wilson, Rodney, 'The Contribution of Muhammad Baqir al-Sadr to Contemporary Islamic Economic Thought', *Journal of Islamic Studies*, 91 (1998), pp. 46-60.

Yusrī, Aḥmad, *Ḥuqūq al-Insān wa Asbāb al-ᶜUnf fi'l-Mujtamaᶜ al-Islāmī fī Ḍaw' Aḥkām al-Sharīᶜah*, Alexandria (Egypt): Mansha'at al-Maᶜārif, 1993.

Al-Zuḥaylī, Wahbah, *al-Fiqh al-Islāmī wa Adillatuhu*, 3rd edn, 8 vols., Damascus: Dār al-Fikr, 1409/1989.

——*Ḥaqq al-Ḥurriyyah fi'l-ᶜĀlam*, Beirut: Dār al-Fikr al-Muᶜāṣir, 1417/1997.

Index

tajassus, *63*
takāful al-ijtimāʿī, 97
taklīf, 43
taqwā, 45, 52
taslīm, 62
trust, 56
trustee, 55

Ukhuwwah, 72
ʿUmar b. ʿAbd al-ʿAzīz, 60
ʿUmar b. al-Khaṭṭāb, 45, 59, 63, 84, 100
ummah, xiii, 32, 55, 99
Umm al-Ḥārith b. Abī Rabīʿa, 2
UNESCO, x
United Nations, x, xii
United States, xii
uṣūl al-fiqh, 55, 92, 94
ulū al-amr, xiii
ʿulamā', xiv, 26, 90, 93, 97

Vicegerency, xiii
vicegerent, 37

wakālah, 55
wakīl, 55
walī, 21, 30
waʿẓ, 41
wealth, 91
Weeramantry, 28
World Health Organisation, xii

Yusrī, Aḥmad, 1

al-Ẓāhirī, 98
Zainuddin, Daim, xii
zakāh, 95, 96, 98, 100
ẓann, 74
ẓann al-mubāḥ, 74
zinā, 90
al-Zuḥaylī, 2
ẓulm, 59